Dallas & Fort Worth

A Pictorial Celebration

Michael Duty

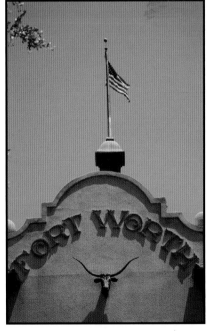

Photography by Elan Penn

Sterling Publishing Co., Inc.
New York

Design by Michel Opatowski
Edited by Jacqueline Mulhern
Layout by Ariane Rybski

Penn Publishing gratefully acknowledges the following institutions and individuals for allowing photographs from their collections to be reproduced in this book:

ADAGP, Paris 2006 138, 139
African American Museum 45
Amon Carter Museum 137
Bass Performance Hall 134
Bill Winfrey, photographer, Tom Dillard Collection, The Dallas Morning News/The Sixth Floor Museum at Dealey Plaza 21
Brad Newton 98
Carolyn Brown 42, 44, 46, 47, 48, 49, 50, 51
Cathy Burkey/Dallas Zoological Society 121
Collegiate Images 52
Dallas Heritage Village 30
Dallas Historical Society 6, 7, 9, 10, 11, 12, 13, 14, 15, 16, 17, 18, 23
Dallas World Aquarium/Cindy Harrison 118
David A. Schulz 26
Forever Resorts 123
Ft. Worth Botanic Garden/Pete Vollenweider
Ft. Worth Convention and Visitors Bureau 110, 131, 158
Ft. Worth Museum of Science and History 143
Oscar Williams 143 (top)
Ft. Worth Zoo 150, 151
Getty Images 94, 104, 105
Gittings 83
Hotel Crescent Court, A Rosewood Hotel 67
Hyatt Regency Dallas 68, 69
Icon SMI/Corbis 97
Lone Star Park at Grand Prairie 101
Louis DeLuca/Dallas Morning News/Corbis 99
Nasher Sculpture Center/Tom Jenkins 78, 79
Southern Methodist University 93
Steven Watson/The Sixth Floor Museum at Dealey Plaza 28
The Adolphus Dallas 58, 59
The Dallas Morning News/The Sixth Floor Museum at Dealey Plaza 20
The Magnolia Dallas 56, 57
The Women's Museum 43
Trammell & Margaret Crow Collection of Asian Art 80, 81

Library of Congress Cataloging-in-Publication Data Available

2 4 6 8 10 9 7 5 3 1

Published by Sterling Publishing Co., Inc.
387 Park Avenue South, New York, NY 10016
© 2007 Penn Publishing Ltd.
Distributed in Canada by Sterling Publishing
c/o Canadian Manda Group, 165 Dufferin Street,
Toronto, Ontario, Canada M6K 3H6
Distributed in the United Kingdom by GMC Distribution Services,
Castle Place, 166 High Street, Lewes, East Sussex, England BN7 1XU
Distributed in Australia by Capricorn Link (Australia) Pty. Ltd.
P.O. Box 704, Windsor, NSW 2756, Australia

Sterling ISBN-13: 978-1-4027-2561-6
ISBN-10: 1-4027-2561-2

For information about custom editions, special sales, premium and corporate purchases, please contact Sterling Special Sales Department at 800-805-5489 or specialsales@sterlingpub.com.

Contents

Dallas/Fort Worth Metroplex:
Where the Old West
Converges with the
New South 6

Historic Dallas: A Natural
Crossroads 24

Old Red Museum of Dallas County
  History and Culture 26
Deep Ellum 27
Dealey Plaza, the JFK Memorial, and
  the Sixth Floor Museum 28
Dallas Heritage Village at
  Old City Park 30
Freedman's Cemetery Memorial 32
Swiss Avenue Historic District 34
West End Historic District 36
Bishop Arts District 38
Union Station .39

Inventing Big D:
  Fair Park and the Texas
  Centennial Exposition 40

Hall of State 42
Women's Museum 43
Music Hall at Fair Park 44
African American Museum 45
Age of Steam Railroad Museum 46
Texas Discovery Gardens 47
Texas State Fair 48
Museum of Science and Nature 50
The Cotton Bowl 52

The Heart of Big D:
  Business, Commerce, and
  Government 54

The Magnolia Building and
  the Flying Pegasus 56
Adolphus Hotel 58
J. P. Morgan/Chase Tower 60
Renaissance Tower 61
Bank of America Plaza 62
Bank One Center 63
Thanksgiving Square 64
Farmer's Market 66
The Crescent 67
Reunion Tower .68
Fountain Place .70
Dallas City Hall 71
The Wilson Building 72
Trailing Longhorns Sculpture in
  Pioneer Plaza Park 73

The Art of Big D:
  Cultural Institutions and the
  Halls of Higher Learning 74

Dallas Museum of Art 76
Nasher Sculpture Center 78
Trammell and Margaret Crow Collection of
  Asian Art 80
Morton H. Myerson Symphony Center . . .82
Cathedral Santuario de Guadalupe 84
Latino Cultural Center 86
Texas Woman's University 87
University of Dallas 88
Texas Christian University 89
University of North Texas 90
Southern Methodist University/Meadows
  Museum 91

At Ease in the Metroplex: Sporting and Shopping Venues 94

Texas Stadium 96
Ameriquest Field 98
American Airlines Center 99
Lone Star Park 100
NorthPark Shopping Center 102
Snider Plaza/University Park 103
Texas Motor Speedway 104
Stonebriar Centre Mall/Frisco 106
Highland Park Village 107

Beyond Big D: Attractions in the Metroplex 108

International Terminal D at
    DFW Airport 110
Dallas Arboretum 111
Frontiers of Flight Museum 112
White Rock Lake 114
Lee Park 115
Reverchon Park 116
Six Flags Over Texas 117
Dallas World Aquarium and
    Zoological Garden 118
Dallas Zoo 120
Southfork Ranch 122
The Mustangs at Las Colinas
    Sculpture 124
McKinney Town Square 125
Denton Town Square 126

Way Out West: Cowboys and Culture in Fort Worth 128

Tarrant County Courthouse 130
Fort Worth Water Gardens 131
Sundance Square 132
Nancy Lee and Perry R. Bass
    Performance Hall 134
Amon Carter Museum 136
Kimbell Art Museum 138
Modern Art Museum of Fort Worth 140
Fort Worth Museum of Science and
    History 142
National Cowgirl Museum and
    Hall of Fame 144
Casa Mañana Theater 146
Trinity Trails 147
Fort Worth Botanic Garden 148
Fort Worth Zoo 150
Cowtown Coliseum 152
Grapevine Vintage Railroad 154
Billy Bob's Texas 155
Livestock Exchange Building and
    the Fort Worth Stockyards 156
Sid W. Richardson Collection of
    Western Art 158

Index 159

Dallas/Fort Worth Metroplex: Where the Old West Converges with the New South

Texas has long had a reputation as perhaps the quintessential "Western" destination; Western in the sense of cowboys, ranches, oil and gas wells, and deep blue skies stretching over vast landscapes. Although these features remain a hallmark, a burgeoning cosmopolitan culture is also on display, welcoming visitors upon arrival.

When travelers disembark at the gleaming new International Terminal D in the Dallas/Fort Worth International Airport, they immediately enter a modern and cosmopolitan urban setting with boutiques, fine restaurants, and a wide array of artworks ranging from mosaics by local and international artists set into the floors to paintings depicting the wide open spaces of a more traditional view of Texas to representative pieces on loan from the acclaimed Nasher Sculpture Center. For some, such a setting may be both a surprise and seem somewhat incongruous. To be sure, one can find all of that in Texas and in fact, all of that in fairly close proximity to the new art-festooned international terminal at DFW Airport.

But the modernism of the new terminal is

Commerce Street from the Square, 1890. Even as early as 1890, Dallas's Downtown was beginning to grow with the construction of hotels, stores, and other services. Many grew up around the courthouse, which served as a commercial and business center. This scene of Commerce Street was taken from the perspective of the town square around the courthouse.

Floyd Willard race car at State Fair, 1917. One of the earliest attractions at the State Fair of Texas was racing—both horses and automobiles. Leading drivers from around the country competed at the fair, such as Floyd Willard, shown here in 1917 prior to a race.

also highly appropriate. Dallas and Fort Worth, while firmly rooted in the traditional image of old Texas, are both rapidly growing urban centers, home to high-tech companies that produce innovative new products, world-renowned museums and cultural centers, and an increasingly international population. Today, the region is home to both the old and the new.

Cattle ranches can still be found only a short drive from urban centers. Fields that once contributed to Dallas's status as the "cotton king" of the world have been turned into rapidly growing suburbs linked to Dallas's business center by one of the country's newest and most successful rapid transit systems, the DART. In Fort Worth, the Old West is still on display in the historic Stockyards District on the city's North Side, where rodeos are held each weekend in the appropriately named Cowtown Coliseum and longhorns are still trailed along city streets (although these steers serve as a mere reminder of the city's cowboy heritage for tourists curious to get a close-up view of the sort of life that has spawned countless Hollywood movies), but the city also prides itself on a museum district that is among the nation's finest.

Dallas and Fort Worth, once bitter rivals and even now spirited competitors, while still retaining quite separate and distinct personalities, have converged to form a unique metropolitan region known locally as the Metroplex. Prior to the construction of DFW Airport, no one in either Dallas or Fort Worth had ever heard of the Dallas/Fort Worth Metroplex; the word, in fact, was invented to describe the sort of urban convergence that many civic planners predicted for the area in 1974 when the airport opened. The location for the airport itself had been hammered out through years of sometimes heated negotiations between the political and business leaders of the two cities. Dallas had long been the area's transportation center since the establishment of Love Field, and Fort Worth had long sought to build its own international airport. DFW was the compromise solution, a regional airport located equidistant from each city. Now the third busiest airport in the United States, DFW was built on mostly vacant prairie land, but it soon became the linchpin for development in the entire region. The predictions made by urban planners thirty years ago have been largely fulfilled. Dallas and Fort Worth have grown toward the airport to create a single, dynamic metropolitan area. Some of the old Dallas/Fort Worth rivalry still exists and many of the smaller communities that make up the outlying areas of the Metroplex also retain their own personalities, but it is the region as a whole that many people outside of the area think of when they think of either Dallas or Fort Worth. Those travelers step-ping into Terminal D from cities around the globe are about to enter a truly diverse region, a place where the Old West resides comfortably with the twenty-first century, a place that has always embraced the new and innovative, and a place whose energy and ambition are as big as Texas.

Historic Dallas: A Natural Crossroads

The concept of the Dallas/Fort Worth Metroplex grew out of the notion of establishing an international gateway to north central Texas, the Dallas/Fort Worth Regional Airport. The airport was designed as a modern crossroads, an intersection of commercial and recreational travel routes. Over a century prior to the opening of the DFW airport, and located approximately 20 miles to the east, John Neely Bryan envisioned a settlement at another cross-roads. This one was located at a natural rock ford on the Trinity River, the only crossing for several miles. The crossing formed an intersection between ancient Native American trade routes. No one really knows what Bryan envisioned when he stood on a bluff overlooking the Trinity River in 1839 and surveyed the rolling black land prairie around him. Bryan had scouted the river for miles to locate the natural formation of Austin chalk that allowed a fairly easy crossing of the river. Native Americans had crossed the Trinity at that spot for generations and some say that Bryan intended to open a trading post to take advantage of the already established Indian traces. Bryan had lived with the Cherokees in Arkansas and was familiar with several tribes in the area. Such familiarity would have served him well both with the Native Americans and with settlers who were increasingly moving into the newly formed Republic of Texas.

Bryan may have also had bigger ideas in mind. Born in Fayetteville, Tennessee, in 1810, he had dabbled in a number of business ventures by the time he made his way to Texas. He had studied

Battle of the Alamo scene from the Texas Centennial Exposition, 1936. When Dallas's business and civic leaders first made overtures to the commission overseeing the 100th anniversary celebration of the birth of the Republic of Texas, many people assumed that San Antonio, home to the Alamo, would be the most likely location for the event. Dallas won, but at least the Battle of the Alamo was recreated on a daily basis for the millions of visitors who attended the festivities.

law and opened a practice in Memphis, but after contracting cholera he moved to Arkansas to recover his health. After his stay with the Cherokees he settled for a while in Van Buren, Arkansas, where he tried his hand at real estate speculation and also assisted with the town grid layout. He may have decided that Texas would be fertile ground to found a city of his own while clerking at a trading post on the Red River.

Whatever his notion, Bryan returned to Arkansas from his scouting trip along the Trinity, settled his business dealings in Fort Smith, and

Chuck Wagon Restaurant. Food played a big role in the Texas Centennial Exposition and the subsequent state fairs held at Dallas's Fair Park. Texas's Western heritage was also frequently highlighted; here the two are combined at one location, a restaurant shaped like a frontier chuck wagon.

two years later made his way back to the bluff overlooking the river. This time he was here to stay, and in only a matter of months he was traveling throughout the area lobbying newly arrived settlers to move to his new town site. The town that he founded would be called Dallas. The origin of that name is not clear. Local legends say that it could have been named after George Mifflin Dallas, who was vice president of the United States under President James K. Polk

in 1844, or his brother, Commodore Alexander Dallas, who had been a naval hero in the War of 1812. Other stories claim that Bryan named the town after a friend named Dallas.

Whatever the origin of its name, Dallas grew steadily through the remainder of the nineteenth century, fueled primarily by the arrival of the railroads that allowed the city to become a national marketplace. Cotton became the primary cash crop of area farmers and East Texas in general. Dallas became both a principle shipping terminal and an important processing and warehouse center. The designation of the city of Dallas as the seat of the county of Dallas further cemented the city's role as the focal point of business and commercial dealings in the area. The county courthouse in the city's West End became a focal point that led to the consolidation of passenger and freight rail lines in a single area and the construction of a new central terminal. Warehouses grew up around the station, while the city grew distinctive residential neighborhoods at some distance away. As the neighborhoods developed, so did streetcar lines. Residential and business districts began to

develop their individual characteristics by the turn of the century; stately homes were built along Swiss Avenue in the Munger addition; Deep Ellum grew into a lively jazz and blues incubator; trolleys enabled workers to live and shop in Oak Cliff and work in downtown. Fashionable suburbs like Highland Park drew people increasingly away from the city's center. In short, Dallas evolved into a cosmopolitan city.

Inventing Big D: Fair Park and the Texas Centennial Exposition

While Dallas was busy with its own metamor-

Esplanade at night, 1936. The centerpiece of the Texas Centennial Exposition was the Texas State Building, built as a monument to Texas history. The building now houses the Dallas Historical Society and is known as the Hall of State. During the Centennial, it was lit nightly by a bank of spotlights located behind it.

phosis from prairie village to bustling city, thirty miles to the west, Fort Worth was also developing its identity, culture, and economy. If Dallas's aspirations always pointed to the East in the sense of a desire to emulate and be seen as an equal to the great cities of the North and East, Fort Worth always looked to the West. It started in fact as a fort established as a frontier defense against Native American depredations. Cotton was king in Dallas, but cattle was king in Fort Worth. The great cattle trails that led from South Texas to the rail heads in Kansas or the sprawling ranches of the open range in Montana and Wyoming passed far closer to Fort Worth than Dallas. Once the railroads came to Fort Worth, so did the meatpacking plants making

President Franklin Delano Roosevelt at the Cotton Bowl in 1936. The Texas Centennial Exposition held in 1936 was Dallas's opportunity to present itself in the best possible light to the rest of the world. When it opened, President Franklin Roosevelt was on hand to address the opening day crowds at a special ceremony held in the newly constructed Cotton Bowl.

Law west of the Pecos, Judge Roy Bean Exhibit. Although Dallas has long presented itself as a thoroughly modern city, the legends of the Old West played a large role in the Centennial Exposition. One of Texas's most legendary western figures was Judge Roy Bean, who was known as "the law west of the Pecos." The Pecos River is a long way from Dallas, but Judge Bean's exploits were recounted daily during the centennial.

the city's North Side the terminus for cattle drives, not the distant markets in Kansas. Fort Worth's stockyards became a center for the buying, selling, processing, and shipping of prime beef, a truly Western heritage that has continued until today.

By the 1930s both cities had grown substantially, with Dallas holding the edge in terms of overall population and commercial activity. A definite competitive edge had developed between the two cities, with the leaders of each often touting the advantages of one to the detriment of the other. As plans began to unfold for a statewide celebration of the centennial of the Texas Republic that was born as a separate country in 1836 when it won independence

Midway at Cavalcade Drive, Texas Centennial Exposition. The Midway is still a major attraction at the annual State Fair of Texas. The fair is held on the same grounds where the Texas Centennial Exposition was staged in 1936. Then as today, the many attractions of the Midway proved to be irresistible to the large crowds who visited each day.

from Mexico (inclusion into the United States would not be achieved for another ten years), city leaders in Dallas saw the event as a great opportunity to declare their city's prominence among all Texas cities. Already, many of its citizens were referring to their home as Big D and hosting the biggest party in Texas history, the Centennial Exposition, would be just the way to announce that fact to the rest of the world. Naturally people in Fort Worth did not share

that enthusiasm. The publisher of the *Fort Worth Star-Telegram* and the city's chief booster, Amon Carter, was fond of quoting his friend Will Rogers who reportedly said "Fort Worth is where the West begins and Dallas is where the East peters out."

Such comments only increased the bravado of the Dallas leaders who lobbied fervently for the centennial. In order to win over the centennial commission, Dallas had to beat out other cities that many saw as having a more legitimate claim to the celebration: Austin was the state capital, San Antonio was the home of the Alamo, and Houston was near where the early Texans won their independence at the Battle of San Jacinto. But Dallas did indeed win, perhaps because of sheer bravado, a local hallmark. One often-told story of the Centennial competition is that when Dallas business leader and future mayor R. L. Thornton was told that San Antonio

leaders had promised to build an esplanade as part of the Centennial complex, he responded by saying, "We'll build two esplanades." The story continues that he then asked his colleagues what an esplanade was.

As it turns out, one esplanade was enough. Dallas won the right to host the Centennial Exposition and it raised and spent millions developing Fair Park, already the site of the State Fair, into a true showpiece that attracted

Texas Centennial Exposition Opening Day Parade, 1936. The Texas Centennial Exposition was the biggest celebration ever staged in Dallas, attracting millions of visitors from around the state, the nation, and the world. It all started with a parade through the streets of Downtown Dallas.

millions of visitors to the city in 1936. Over in Fort Worth, Amon Carter presented a rival exposition; true to Fort Worth's roots, he named his the Texas Frontier Centennial Celebration and coined the phrase, "Go to Dallas for education, but come to Fort Worth for fun."

The Heart of Big D: Business, Commerce, and Government

Many people in Dallas may not have completely disagreed with that sentiment, for they have always seen their city in terms of its importance

Stagecoach Holdup, Texas Centennial Exposition, 1936. Just as many visitors do today, people traveling to Dallas to attend the Texas Centennial Exposition expected to get a firsthand look at the Western side of Texas. By 1936, stagecoaches had not been sighted in Dallas for decades, but Centennial visitors could still witness a holdup each day, even if it were only staged for entertainment purposes.

Dallas skyline, looking northeast from the Trinity River. The Dallas skyline has undergone numerous transformations since its founding, with buildings constructed and later torn down to make way for new skyscrapers. One constant has been the barrier that the Trinity River has placed on development south of Downtown, shown here at mid-century. Today plans for the river include extensive park and recreational development that will provide a greenbelt in contrast to the continuing development of the city's center.

as a center for business and finance, a place of commerce, but also of education, culture, and refinement. Dallas has always taken great pride in its stature as a major American city, one that could boast of fine hotels, increasingly grand skyscrapers, elegant residential neighborhoods, and top-rate educational institutions. It is no wonder that many in the city were particularly hard hit when Dallas's reputation went into a free-fall decline following the assassination of

John F. Kennedy in 1963. Ironically, most Dallas leaders had decided to roll out the red carpet for Kennedy to dispel the notion that the city was inhospitable. It would take years for Dallas to recover from the blow to its image that the assassination delivered. In the ensuing decades the city went through great prosperity as evidenced by a proliferation of Class A office buildings designed by leading national and international architects in its downtown core, and

almost complete financial collapse in the 1980s as oil prices tumbled and real estate speculators sank into debt. The decades following World War II were truly a roller coaster of growth, decline, and growth which changed the face of the city on numerous occasions. The 1980s epitomized the boom-and-bust nature of that cycle. It saw the construction of numerous buildings by such world-renowned designers as I. M. Pei and Philip Johnson and the collapse of most of its local banks. By the century's end, the building boom was once again on the upswing.

The Art of Big D: Cultural Institutions and the Halls of Higher Learning

While Dallas was concentrating on being a financial and business center throughout much of the latter half of the twentieth century, Fort Worth was quietly forging an image as a cultural center. Underneath its aura as a "cowtown," Fort Worth was also becoming known for world-class museums designed by famous architects. Philip Johnson began the trend with the Amon Carter Museum and was quickly followed by Louis Kahn who designed the Kimbell Art Museum, still seen as one of the world's great pieces of museum architecture over 30 years after its completion. The prestigious international Van Cliburn piano competition added to the city's cultural legacy.

While somewhat overshadowed by these developments in the 1960s and 1970s, by the 1980s Dallas began to pay greater and greater attention to its cultural facilities as well. A multi-million-dollar city bond election allowed the Dallas Museum of Art to build a new Edward Barnes–designed building in the heart of Downtown Dallas as the first anchor of a new urban Arts District. The Morton H. Meyerson Symphony Center, designed by I. M. Pei, opened

to great acclaim a few years later, followed in more recent years by the Nasher Sculpture Center, the Trammell and Margaret Crow Collection of Asian Art, and recently the huge Dallas Center for the Performing Arts, all within walking distance of one another. In terms of sheer numbers, few cities rival Dallas in terms of notable cultural facilities designed by acclaimed architects.

At Ease in the Metroplex: Sporting and Shopping Venues

While business, art, and culture are important elements in any city's growth and atmosphere, leisure amenities such as sporting venues and shopping centers can equally define a city's character. Dallas and Fort Worth have always placed major significance on sports, particularly football, which some say borders on fanaticism. All of the area universities emphasize their athletic departments, and historically both cities have taken great pride in such events as the annual New Year's Day Cotton Bowl football game. In addition, few football rivalries in the country can match the intensity of the annual contest between the University of Texas and the University of Oklahoma held during the State Fair each October; that event has become something of a local cultural phenomenon.

Despite the popularity of these collegiate events (in fact even high school football has an avid fan base in the area), the real spotlight is turned on the area's professional teams, baseball's Texas Rangers, basketball's Dallas Mavericks, the National Hockey League's Dallas Stars and especially the Dallas Cowboys. These last started out playing games in Fair Park's venerable Cotton Bowl, but moved into their own stadium in Irving in 1971. Many people in Dallas are absolutely convinced that the

Cowboys' ascendancy in terms of national popularity beginning in the 1970s was as important as any other factor in finally reversing the city's tarnished image due to the Kennedy assassination. Certainly the Cowboys and their acclaimed cheerleaders have done much to make Dallas a household name throughout the country in a positive way.

Sports are a big business in the Dallas/Fort Worth area, but so is another leisure activity which some people pursue with equal fervor—shopping. Dallas is a shopping and fashion center with numerous high-end centers, boutiques, and malls. NorthPark, developed in the early 1960s by Ray Nasher, is perhaps the city's quintessential shopping destination with such flagship stores as Neiman-Marcus and examples from Nasher's world-class collection of contemporary sculpture on display throughout the center. NorthPark may be the largest, but it is by no means isolated in terms of other shopping venues available throughout the area. Since the early days of both cities, people have traveled to Dallas and Fort Worth to trade goods and shop. As the Metroplex has steadily grown, this activity has not diminished in the least.

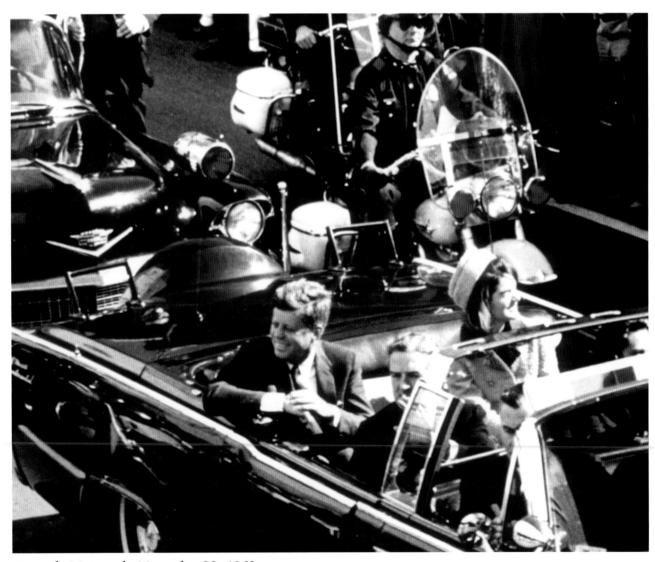

Kennedy Motorcade, November 22, 1963.

Lee Harvey Oswald escorted by Detective Elmer Boyd through the police station hallway shortly after his arrest.

Beyond Big D: Attractions in the Metroplex

Perhaps one of the most interesting developments in the recent history of Dallas and Fort Worth is that the area really has substantially grown beyond both the geographic limitations and the individual personalities of both cities. Today Dallas/Fort Worth is more than the simple sum of the two cities; it is a region that has many distinctive cities to be sure, but also a region that in many ways acts as a single entity covering 8,991 square miles. The Dallas Cowboys play in Irving and will soon call Arlington home. The Texas Rangers draw fans from both cities and the surrounding area to their home field in Arlington. Shoppers from Fort Worth can find their favorite stores in the suburb of Southlake. Workers in Downtown Dallas ride DART to their homes in Frisco. Denton and McKinney were once small cities to the north of Dallas and

Fort Worth today; they are bedroom communities with booming populations. An increasing number people who live here consider themselves to be residents of the Metroplex as much as residents of any particular city.

The Metroplex has mushroomed into a major population center. The 2005 U. S. Census Bureau reports the population as 5,819,475, while the North Central Texas Council of Governments estimates the current 2006 population to be just over 6,000,000. Using census bureau figures, the racial breakdown is white or Caucasian–58%, Hispanic–21% (the fastest growing ethnic group projected to be the single largest group in 10 years), African-American–14%, Native-American–1%, Asian and Hawaiian–4%, two or more races–2%.

That trend toward a regional identity may have begun in earnest in the early 1960s, when such entertainment venues as Six Flags Over Texas opened midway between Dallas and Fort Worth in Arlington, creating a destination that drew equally between both cities. Given the development of our modern dependency on the automobile and a first-class highway system, area residents have become accustomed to ranging throughout the entire region for both work and recreation. People in Dallas easily travel to Fort Worth to visit the Kimbell and natives from Fort Worth just as easily take in the live music scene in Dallas's Deep Ellum district. Travelers from across the country may descend upon the Metroplex in search of the mythical Dallas of the popular television show, but what they find is a large, increasingly complex and diverse region that is composed of many different communities.

Way Out West: Cowboys and Culture in Fort Worth

While the Metroplex steadily grows toward Oklahoma, many people in Dallas still cling to the notion of Big D. For them, Dallas is still a place of infinite possibility with the next big development, the next big opportunity for fame and fortune just around the corner. In many ways, Dallas has always looked toward the future and has been adept at shedding the outdated baggage of the past. Some would say that tendency has led to a less-than-stellar record in terms of historic preservation, but in more recent years there seems to be a greater concern for the past. While the city moves forward with ambitious new developments like Victory, it has also taken steps to protect the nearby West End Historic District. The Arts District boasts brand new facilities but has also preserved such shrines as the Cathedral Santuario de Guadalupe.

Over in Fort Worth, the new and the old have coincided for many years. In fact, the city has actively promoted its "cowboys and culture" theme for decades. The Old West is on display daily in the historic Stockyards section of the North Side of Fort Worth, while cutting-edge modern art is equally accessible at the Modern Art Museum in the Museum District. The Nancy Lee and Perry R. Bass Performance Hall in Sundance Square is located across the street from the historic Tarrant County Courthouse. Philip Johnson's Water Gardens anchors one end of Downtown Fort Worth while the paintings of Western artists Frederic Remington and Charles Russell reside at the other end in the Sid W. Richardson Collection of Western Art museum. Fort Worth is at once an ultra-modern cultural center and a throwback to the days of cowboys and cattle drives, and its residents seem entirely comfortable with that arrangement.

It is perhaps this dual nature, frontier history mingled with contemporary art, which is certainly exemplified by the juxtaposition of Henry Moore's *Dallas Piece* only a stone's throw from Robert Summers' *Trailing Longhorns* near Dallas City Hall and the Convention Center, that may be the lasting impression that travelers will take with them as they leave the Metroplex from the new Terminal D at the Dallas/Fort Worth International Airport. They may have

Dallas skyline in the 1930s. As Dallas prepared to host the world at the Texas Centennial Exposition in 1936, its downtown had grown to be one of the busiest business centers in the Southwest. Dallasites were proud of the growth of their city and were pleased to tout the city as "Big D."

received well more than they bargained for when they first arrived. The Dallas/Fort Worth area has its oil wells and cattle ranches, but it also has its share of contemporary art and new technology, which makes for a dynamic place to live in the new century.

While residents have long enjoyed the Metroplex's attractions, travelers increasingly appreciate its charms. In 2003, the area was the number one vacation destination in Texas, according to the Dallas Fort Worth Area Tourism Council. Visitors added $14 billion to the local economy that year, as well as 142,000 jobs with

an annual payroll of $5.3 billion. Local and state taxes of $855 million were collected solely from tourism. In this sector of the local economy, the nickname "Big D" may stand for "Big Dollars" as well as "Big Dallas."

Historic Dallas:
A Natural Crossroads

Old Red Museum of Dallas County History and Culture

When Dallas County was officially carved out of neighboring counties in 1846 by the newly established state legislature, the city of Dallas was not the official county seat. After winning independence from Mexico, Texas was originally established as a separate, independent republic in 1836 and did not enter the United States as a state until 1845. Hord's Ridge (now known as Oak Cliff) and Cedar Springs (now known as Oak Lawn) also had aspirations for the honor. In an effort to bolster Dallas's claim as county seat, its founding citizen, John Neely Bryan, and his new wife, Margaret Beeman, donated land near their cabin to serve as a site for a permanent county courthouse. The first four attempts to build a courthouse were hardly permanent. One of the buildings was condemned as unsafe shortly after it was built, and others burned. The fifth courthouse to be built on the Bryan-donated site has stood the test of time.

Affectionately known as "Old Red" because of the color of its Pecos sandstone, the building was begun in 1890 and completed in 1893. Designed by M. A. Orlopp in what has been called a Richardson (after noted courthouse architect H. H. Richardson) Romanesque style, the building became the center of the young city's commercial and business district, as well as the local seat of government. In the ensuing century since it was built, the building has gone through numerous changes that greatly altered its original design. Its massive clock tower was removed in 1919 for safety reasons. A combination of the weight and the strength of the North Texas winds had weakened it to the point that officials feared it would tumble down with the next big storm.

Scarlet-clad Marines march past the Old Red Courthouse in Downtown Dallas as part of Dallas's annual Veteran's Day Parade. Completed in 1893, the sandstone and granite landmark occupies the original city block deeded to the county by Dallas founder John Neely Bryan. The building, which has undergone a complete restoration, will reopen in 2007 as the home of Old Red Museum of Dallas County History and Culture.

Previous page: Railroad depot, Dallas Heritage Village at Old City Park. This depot, built in 1886 at Fate, Texas, is typical of the board-and-batten construction used by the Missouri-Kansas-Texas Railroad, better known as the Katy, during the period.

Deep Ellum

Deep Ellum is located just east of Downtown Dallas and is bounded by Main, Commerce, Canton, and Elm streets. Its name is derived from the latter street. Deep Ellum has gone through many incarnations since the early days of Dallas. It was one of the original neighborhoods where African-Americans settled following the Civil War. Later it became one of the city's first industrial warehouse districts with the establishment of both a Ford assembly plant and a large plant for the production of cotton gins.

In the decades prior to and just after World War I, Deep Ellum was a center for jazz and blues in the South. It was home to countless clubs and music venues where such legendary performers as Blind Lemon Jefferson, Huddie "Leadbelly" Ledbetter, and Robert Johnson regularly entertained. One of Johnson's last records was cut in a studio in Deep Ellum.

The lively nightlife of the neighborhood went into steep decline when the construction of the Central Expressway in the late 1940s cut the neighborhood off from the rest of Downtown Dallas. For several years afterward, Deep Ellum was left to deteriorate, and its status as a desirable entertainment district was replaced with a reputation as one of the city's most dangerous spots.

Beginning in the late 1970s, Deep Ellum's fortunes changed once again. Artists and musicians came to the area's rescue by transforming the vacant warehouses and buildings into studios, lofts, and nightclubs.

Since then the neighborhood has had both good times and bad, but today it is again a center for live music and entertainment with several clubs, restaurants, and galleries. Just as in the 1920s, Deep Ellum is relatively quiet during the day, but its music scene rocks far into the night.

Dealey Plaza, the JFK Memorial, and the Sixth Floor Museum

John F. Kennedy Memorial.

Without question the most infamous and tragic event to occur in all of Dallas's history was the assassination of President John F. Kennedy on November 22, 1963. Ironically, Kennedy was shot only a few yards from the original home of Dallas's founder, John Neely Bryan. The President was riding in an open limousine that had just passed the Old Red Courthouse and turned onto Elm Street in front of the building that housed the Texas School Book Depository. Fatal shots were fired from a sixth-story window by Lee Harvey Oswald. Two days later, Oswald himself was shot and killed by Jack Ruby while being transferred from a city jail to a county facility. Seven years later a memorial, designed by noted architect Philip Johnson, was dedicated to the fallen president. Twenty-five years later, the Sixth Floor Museum opened in the building where Oswald had fired; and today over two million visitors a year visit the Dealey Plaza area.

Not all visit the museum or the memorial. Some simply wander around the area, talking with or avoiding the many conspiracy theorists who are always willing to share their particular theories on the assassination. The memorial has been somewhat controversial from the beginning. Some people are critical of its rather somber and Spartan design. Johnson, who was a Kennedy family friend, conceived the memorial as a cenotaph, or open tomb. It is constructed of concrete, steel, and marble, fifty feet square and thirty feet in height. The memorial is located across the street from the Old Red Courthouse and adjacent to the Sixth Floor Museum, which has assumed responsibility for interpreting the site.

Sixth Floor Museum.

28

While the memorial is spare and understated, the museum, which is located on the sixth and seventh floors of the building, now home to Dallas county offices, provides a thorough, comprehensive, and thoughtful multimedia presentation not only on the details of the assassination, but also on the history of the times, and the political and cultural climate of Dallas and the rest of the nation during that period. The permanent exhibition on Kennedy and the events surrounding his assassination is found on the sixth floor, including a recreation of the area where Oswald discharged his weapon. The seventh floor of the museum is devoted to changing exhibitions that focus on the history of the times. The museum is one of the most attended in the area with an annual visitation of more than 400,000 people.

Dealey Plaza itself is located at the convergence of Elm, Main, and Commerce streets at Houston Street, just west of Downtown. The plaza was constructed in the 1930s as a Public Works Administration project to address the continuing problem of flood control in the Trinity River Basin. It was named in honor of George Bannerman Dealey, the founding publisher of the *Dallas Morning News* and a longtime civic leader. His bronze statue faces the courthouse. The plaza is in close proximity to John Neely Bryan's original claim that led to the founding of the city. In short, much of the history of Dallas can be told in this relatively small area, stretching from the city's origin to its most unfortunate occurrence up to today. Only

Dealey Plaza.

a short distance from the plaza and the museum that commemorates the life and death of John Kennedy sits the gleaming new development of Victory Park, home to the American Airlines Center, several upscale hotels and condominiums, as well as a host of retail shops and restaurants. If Dealey Plaza can be said to reflect upon Dallas's past, then Victory Park projects Dallas's future.

Dallas Heritage Village at Old City Park

Located just a short distance from the intersection of Interstate Highways 30 and 35, south of the bustle of Downtown Dallas, is a thirteen-acre park; in fact it is the site of the city's first public park. Here visitors can get a firsthand and first-person look at the history of Dallas from the 1840s to 1901. Dallas Heritage Village is composed of thirty-eight structures, ranging from a one-room school house built in 1888 to a 1906 working print shop to a 1930s-era bank, providing the backdrop to North Texas's largest living history museum. Costumed

Right: Nip and Tuck, Dallas Heritage Village's Mammoth Jack donkeys, transport visitors around the museum grounds in a carriage.

Below: Renner School was built in 1888 to serve the rural community of Renner, Texas, just north of Dallas. Grades one to five met in the classroom downstairs, while grades six and seven met upstairs, in the "high school." The original gray paint on the walls, windows, and door trim remains, along with the blackboards (just boards painted black). The Renner School was moved to Dallas Heritage Village in 1975.

At the Living Farmstead, it is always 1861. At Dallas Heritage Village, visitors may see Mrs. Kennedy knitting a sweater from the wool of the Farmstead's sheep or Erastus Rausch hoeing one of his two vegetables gardens. The "dog trot" style log house, common throughout the South, invites old and young alike to experience life in 1861 with all their senses—including touch—when they walk through each room.

interpreters can be found in many of the structures to give visitors a glimpse of life in each particular era. A Civil War–era farm affords children and adults the opportunity to sample the daily chores of a household on the North Texas prairie complete with a vegetable garden and livestock.

The costumed interpreters at Dallas Heritage Village embody fictional characters representing a composite of people who would have been found at each location and era. Visitors can engage each actor in conversation to learn more about life at that time, but each interpreter is only aware of the year that he or she represents.

It is always 1861 at the Kennedy farm and always 1901 at the Blum household. The days and months change depending upon when one visits, but the years do not.

Dallas Heritage Village began in the 1960s as the Dallas County Heritage Society and was formed to preserve a single structure, Millermore House, one of Dallas's grandest homes in the nineteenth century. The Village has grown over the years and is now an accredited museum by the American Association of Museums. In addition to tours and living history presentations, the Village offers classes, workshops, and many other educational activities year round.

Freedman's Cemetery Memorial

In recent years, Uptown Dallas, which is located north of Downtown and east of Central Expressway (U.S. Highway 75), has become a hotspot for high-end development. Neighborhoods such as the State-Thomas area are now home to trendy restaurants, condominiums, and upscale apartment complexes. Shortly after the Civil War, this area was largely an African-American settlement. Many recently freed slaves lived, worked, and worshipped in the area. They were also buried there in a freedman's cemetery.

In the mid 1990s, a major expansion of the Central Expressway was slated to pass directly through a portion of the cemetery, necessitating the removal of several graves. The construction of the freeway also uncovered a number of historic artifacts that tied directly to the original African-American settlement. Federal and state funds were appropriated to recover the items (many of which are now at the African American Museum in Fair Park), move the grave sites to a new cemetery adjacent to the freeway, and create a lasting memorial to the lives of these early pioneer settlers of Dallas.

Entrance to the memorial.

Dream of Freedom *by sculptor David Newton.*

An arched granite gate welcomes visitors to the cemetery. Sculptor David Newton has created several pieces that relate to African history and religion and symbolize the transition from African culture to African-American culture. A Freedman's Cemetery Memorial Foundation has now been formed to provide funds for the maintenance of the cemetery and for the placement of additional works of art.

Swiss Avenue Historic District

Stretching just east of Downtown Dallas, Swiss Avenue in Old East Dallas is a reminder of one of Dallas's most elegant eras and stands as an example of neighborhood revitalization. Much of Old East Dallas was settled by French and Swiss immigrants who originally came to the area in the 1850s to establish a utopian colony, La Reunion.

The colony quickly failed but many of the craftsmen and artisans decided to stay in Dallas, giving the city one of its first cultural bases. Swiss Avenue was named by Dr. Henri Boll, who had first settled in Texas at Galveston after leaving his native Switzerland. The avenue was part of one of Dallas's first exclusive neighborhood developments, Munger Place. Over a short period of time in the late nineteenth and early twentieth centuries, Swiss Avenue became home to over 100 mansions, many in the distinctive Prairie School style.

By the 1970s, however, many of those houses had fallen on hard times and were badly in need of repair. Many houses along neighboring Gaston Avenue already had been torn down to construct a row of apartment buildings. To combat such a fate for Swiss Avenue, neighborhood activists organized and petitioned the city to designate portions of Swiss Avenue, Bryan Parkway, and La Vista and Bryan streets as an historic district, one of the first such districts in the city. That designation was granted in 1973, and in 1974 the district was placed on the National Register of Historic Places.

Renovation and restoration of the homes in the district are now carefully monitored to ensure historic standards. Unlike many other Dallas neighborhoods, where older houses are routinely torn down and replaced with "McMansions," construction in the Swiss Avenue Historic District is regulated, thus assuring the preservation of this diverse architectural heritage.

Although not in the historic district, the other end of Swiss Avenue near Downtown has also undergone preservation efforts. Led by the Meadows Foundation, several vintage homes and buildings have been restored and now serve as offices for numerous nonprofit organizations.

West End Historic District

During the latter part of the nineteenth and early years of the twentieth centuries, Dallas quickly developed into a market and manufacturing center for North Texas, largely due to the arrival of several railroads. The Houston and Central Texas Railway ran along what is now Central Expressway, forming a north/south axis connecting the city to the burgeoning markets of St. Louis and Chicago. The Texas and Pacific Railway ran through the city on an east/west route. Other rail lines soon linked up with those primary routes and the West End of Dallas became a bustling area of red brick warehouses and manufacturing centers that produced a wide variety of goods that could then be easily shipped via the nearby railroads. The area was also near the seat of county govern-

ment and the main railroad passenger terminal, making it one of the most active areas of the city. That hustle and bustle lasted as long as the railroad was the primary means of moving goods in and out of Dallas. By the mid-twentieth century, cars and trucks had replaced railroads as the chief means of moving freight, and the warehouses of the West End gradually were abandoned.

By the early 1980s, however, the district had become a model of adaptive reuse. Restaurants, clubs, and shopping centers replaced factories and distribution centers. The entire 36-block area is now on the National Register of Historic Places and the district encompasses several museums and the Dallas World Aquarium and Zoological Garden.

The West End has become a favorite spot for tourists, but it is once again going through a transformation. The nearby Victory Park development with its high-rise hotels and the American Airlines Center has dampened the popularity of the old warehouse district somewhat.

The district is still home to many annual events, such as the Taste of Dallas, which offers samples from some of Dallas's finest restaurants. The Friday night prior to the annual football game between the Longhorns of the University of Texas and the Sooners of the University of Oklahoma attracts some 30,000 fans from both schools to the district for pregame pep rallies.

The recent addition of the House of Blues to the historic White Swan Building has also added another entertainment anchor to the area.

Bishop Arts District

In the very early days of Dallas, the area south of the Trinity River was a separate town, first called Hord's Ridge, named after the city's founder, and later Oak Cliff. When the city of Dallas was named the county seat of Dallas County, Oak Cliff was a mere 28 votes away from that designation itself. A few years later, Dallas annexed Oak Cliff, this time by only 18 votes. As a South Dallas neighborhood, Oak Cliff has seen both times of prosperity and less robust economic fortunes. In recent years, many areas of the neighborhood have once again enjoyed a rebound, much of it driven by historic renovation both in housing and retail developments.

A prime example is the Bishop Arts District, a collection of approximately 40 early twentieth-century buildings located along Bishop Avenue in north Oak Cliff. The trolley arrived in this area in 1904 and a shopping district quickly grew up around the stop. Up until the 1930s, the stop was one of the busiest in Dallas. Once automobiles took the place of streetcars and trains, the area around the Bishop Street stop and in fact much of Oak Cliff declined. Beginning in the 1970s, the neighborhood began a resurgence, and several pioneering investors rehabilitated the buildings that were still in relatively good condition. Gradually, restaurants, art galleries, and unique boutiques opened. Today there is even talk of restoring the old trolley tracks and creating a modern version of the streetcar line. The area also boasts one of the city's most unique art experiments. Many of the buildings are decorated with colorful, large murals that depict the history of the area, all done by high school students who won the right to participate in mural painting classes and then to put their own versions of Oak Cliff history on the walls.

One of the many colorful, large murals that depict the history of the area.

Union Station

Prior to 1916, when the Beaux-Arts-style Union Station designed by Chicago architect Jarvis Hunt was built, Dallas could boast of having five rail passenger terminals. The situation was hardly practical and most inconvenient for travelers who may have arrived on one railroad and had to make their way to a completely different station to continue their journey. The opening of Union Station consolidated all of the passenger rail service in Dallas into one location at the southwestern edge of Downtown. The terminal could and often did accommodate 100 trains a day and as many as 80,000 passengers, making it one of the busiest stations in the entire Southwest.

As passenger train service diminished, the station became less active. It even served as a temporary home to the Dallas Public Library in the 1950s during construction of a new facility. Even with a decline in train travel, the terminal has continued to serve its original purpose of consolidating passenger service. Today three different types of train travel are available at the station. Amtrak provides both north/south and east/west routes on a national scale, while the Trinity Railway Express operates commuter service between Downtown Fort Worth and Downtown Dallas. In addition, Union Station is a primary depot for the Dallas Area Rapid Transit (DART) system, which provides light rail service to a large and increasing area of Dallas. While service does not number in the hundreds of trains on a daily basis, the terminal nonetheless still remains quite active for both tourists and residents.

Inventing Big D:
Fair Park and the Texas
Centennial Exposition

Designed as the centerpiece of the Texas Centennial Exposition held in 1936 to commemorate the 100th anniversary of Texas's independence from Mexico, the Hall of State was originally known as the Texas State Building. Built at a cost of $1.3 million, it was the grandest of all the 26 buildings built for Texas's version of a World's Fair. At the time, the building was the most expensive per square foot of any building in the entire state. It was situated at the end of a grand esplanade that included a lagoon and lighted fountains. The building is clad in native Texas limestone; in fact all of the materials inside and outside of the building are native to Texas.

In the years leading up to the Centennial, several cities vied for the honor of hosting the event. During the depths of the Depression, the notion of spending $25 million even on the grandest of all state celebrations was a daunting proposition for any city in the state. However, Dallas, led by civic booster R. L. Thornton (now honored with a statue in front of the Hall of State), forged ahead by virtually guaranteeing that the city would come up with any money necessary beyond what the state could afford to make the Centennial a success.

The area chosen for the celebration, Fair Park, had already been the site for the annual State Fair of Texas since the late 1880s, and many buildings that could be utilized for the event were already in place. Dallas architect George Dahl was selected to oversee the project. He engaged ten architectural firms to complete the project in less than two years. Today many of the buildings built for the exposition still remain and are used for a variety of purposes. Dahl designed the exposition as an expression of both Art Deco and Southwestern styles. The result of their work is one of the largest collections of Art Deco buildings anywhere in the country. The entire Fair Park area is now on the National Register of Historic Places.

Sometimes referred to as the Westminster Abbey of Texas, the Hall of State has been home to the Dallas Historical Society since 1938 and contains the Society's 1.5 million–item archives and research library. The building consists of the semicircular Hall of Heroes, which features larger-than-life bronze statues of six heroes from the Republic era: Stephen Austin, James Fannin, Thomas J. Rusk, Mirabeau B. Lamar, Sam Houston, and William B. Travis. The Hall of Heroes leads to the Great Hall that houses two immense murals of Texas history. Four galleries, each devoted to a specific region of the state, flank the Hall of Heroes.

Built in the State of Texas for the 1936 Centennial Exposition, the Hall of State has hosted events honoring presidents, royalty, heads of state, and other dignitaries for over sixty years.

Previous page: Dallas City Hall Plaza.

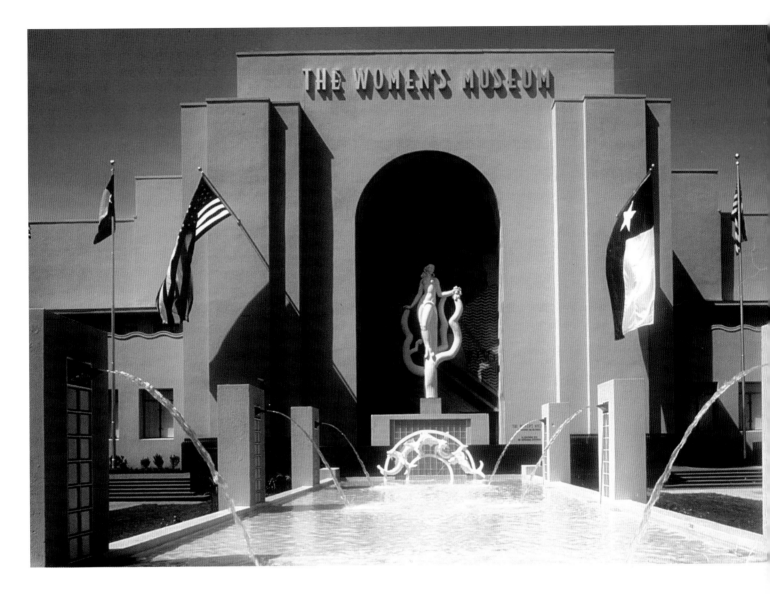

Women's Museum

The newest museum in Fair Park is located in one of its oldest buildings. Built in 1910 as one of Dallas's first coliseums, the building that would eventually house a high-tech institution devoted to women's history has served many different purposes. It was the first building that George Dahl chose to refurbish when he began the Texas Centennial Exhibition project and it housed the administration building for it. Later, the building performed a similar function for the State Fair Association. However, by the mid-1990s the building was in serious disrepair and in danger of being torn down as unsafe. Cathy Bonner, the founder of the Women's Museum, saw the structure in 1996 when she was scouting sites in several cities to build a museum that she envisioned would chronicle the many contribu-

tions that women had made to world history. When Dahl adapted the building for the Centennial, he commissioned sculptor Raul Josset to create a signature piece for the building's entry. The sculpture depicted a young woman rising from a cactus and was entitled *The Spirit of the Centennial*. Bonner was captivated by the sculpture and thought the building would be an appropriate home for the museum she envisioned.

Anchored by a $10 million donation by SBC Communications Inc., the museum opened in 2000, featuring such innovative teaching tools as electronic conversations with great women of the past. Subtitled "An Institute for the Future," the museum places great emphasis on education and preparing young women for leadership roles.

The Fair Park Music Hall was built in 1925 and designed by Lang & Witchell. The design incorporates Spanish Colonial revival with dominating square towers. Home to the Dallas Summer Musicals, the Dallas Opera, and the Texas Ballet Theatre, the Music Hall attracts large crowds seeking top-level entertainment.

Music Hall at Fair Park

Not every building in Fair Park is an example of Art Deco style. Some, like the Music Hall, actually predate the Centennial. Built in 1925, and renovated in 1954 to add air conditioning, the Music Hall at Fair Park has a distinctive Spanish style and is located just inside the main gates of the park. It is the home of Dallas Summer Musicals, the Dallas Opera (which is slated to move to the new Dallas Center for the Performing Arts in a few years), and the Texas Ballet Theater. It has also been the site for numerous concert performances that have ranged from classical to rock.

The Music Hall was enlarged in 1972 to include 3,420 seats and refurbished once again in 1999. It is managed by the DSM Management Group, which also manages the historic Majestic Theater nearby in Downtown Dallas. DSM brings several Broadway productions to both venues throughout the year. The Group has developed an innovative way of assuring that many popular productions include Dallas on their touring schedule; they are early financial backers of the shows. Among the shows that the group has helped finance are *Wicked* and the musical version of *The Lord of the Rings Trilogy*.

One of the most popular attractions at the 1936 Texas Centennial Exposition in terms of attendance was also one of the most controversial, the Hall of Negro Life. When the centennial was being planned, no funds were originally set aside for an exhibition hall that would focus on the history and accomplishments of African-Americans. Dallas's African-American leaders had lobbied the state commission repeatedly and unsuccessfully to include the Hall in its plans. Finally the Dallas Negro Chamber of Commerce won federal funds to create the facility. The building, designed by architect George Dahl, featured art exhibitions and historical displays; an outdoor amphitheater was the sight of daily musical and dramatic performances. A year after the Centennial Exposition closed, another exposition, the Texas and Greater Pan American Exposition, opened, but the Hall of Negro Life was nowhere to be found. It was the first building razed following the Centennial.

Fifty-seven years later near the same the location, the African American Museum opened to celebrate African-American culture and history. The museum was founded in 1974 as part of Bishop College. The museum has both art and history exhibits and contains one of the country's largest collections of African-American folk art. It is visited by more than 100,000 people yearly.

The African American Museum has both art and history exhibits and contains one of the country's largest collections of African-American folk art.

Age of Steam Railroad Museum

One can argue that Dallas would not be anywhere near the metropolitan center it is if the railroads had not come to and through the city early in its history. Their presence turned what could have been a small trading post on the Texas prairie into a bustling market center. Much of that early rail history can be relived at the Age of Steam Railroad Museum, which was started in 1963 and now features several examples of rolling stock from a wide range of historic periods. The museum features both steam and diesel locomotives, as well as the entire 1903 Houston and Texas Central Pacific depot. The Houston and Texas Central Pacific line ran along what is now the city's Central Freeway.

The museum also features passenger cars and an elegant dining car where dinners for museum patrons and members are still held. Many of America's legendary rail lines and routes are represented at the museum, including the Santa Fe and the Union Pacific.

One of the rarest attractions that is not specifically related to Dallas history, but certainly is important to railroad history, is one of only eight surviving "Big Boys," the largest and most powerful steam locomotives built. Engine 4018

The railroad engines and passenger cars exhibited at the Age of Steam Museum at Fair Park recall for visitors the era when the railroads made Dallas the transportation center of North Texas.

was commissioned by the Union Pacific Railroad in 1942 to pull freight over a particularly difficult grade near Laramie, Wyoming. It is now part of the permanent collection of the museum and can be seen daily.

"Big Tex" has welcomed visitors to the State Fair of Texas every year since 1952. Wearing 70-gallon boots and a 75-gallon hat, "Tex" towers to a height of 52 feet.

exhibits featuring the latest automobiles, the latest kitchen gadgets, carnival rides on the Midway, a nightly parade capped off by a computerized light show, and the largest and perhaps strangest array of fried foods offered anywhere at any event. If it can be deep fried and consumed, whether it is an Oreo cookie or a peanut butter, jelly, and banana sandwich, it more than likely has been sold at the Texas State Fair.

The fair starts the last weekend in September and runs for the following three weeks. Traditional highlights include the annual football showdown between the University of Texas and the University of Oklahoma, played during the fair since 1929 and a perennial sell-out. "Big Tex," a 52-foot cowboy, has been dispensing information about daily events since 1952 and has become the universal symbol of the fair, and some would say of Dallas itself.

Museum of Science and Nature

In 2006, two venerable and popular Fair Park institutions joined forces to create a new museum devoted to all forms of scientific inquiry, exploration, and investigation. Together, the museums account for well over 500,000 visitors each year, and both have operated large and well-orchestrated educational programs.

Now operating as a single entity, the museums combine wide-ranging resources in terms of collections and services. The new museum is the Museum of Science and Nature, a product of a merger between the Dallas Museum of Natural History and The Science Place.

The Dallas Museum of Natural History began with the Centennial in 1936. It features one of the state's largest natural history collections that numbers over 280,000 items that stretch over

The Fair Park Science Place provides varied programs for learning about science. Such programs include dual-language immersion programs, hands-on curriculum, science enrichment, and exhibits portraying the wonders of our world.

millions of years of earth history. On permanent display are extensive dioramas that depict native Texas flora and fauna. The museum also features changing exhibitions throughout the year. In recent years, the museum has been especially active in research and exhibitions relating to dinosaurs.

The Science Place is located in two buildings and includes over 200 interactive exhibits. It has an IMAX theater and a planetarium. The museum began in 1946 as the Dallas Health Museum. In 1983, it moved into the building that formerly had been occupied by the Dallas Museum of Fine Arts after that museum relocated to the Downtown Arts District.

The new museum is currently conducting a capital campaign to build a 200,000 square-foot museum in close proximity to the Arts District itself. The new museum will continue to occupy its Fair Park property even after the new building is completed for educational and collection activities.

The Cotton Bowl

The Cotton Bowl refers to the name of both the stadium and the annual college football game played there each New Year's Day (on a few occasions the game has been played on the day before or after January 1). The stadium is located just behind the Hall of State and was built in 1930, prior to the Texas Centennial Exposition. At one time, Southern Methodist University played its home games there, a decision prompted by the tremendous popularity of Doak Walker, a three-time All-American, and winner of the Heisman Trophy. He was a star running back for the Detroit Lions, and most importantly for Dallas fans, a native of the city. So many fans wanted to see Walker play that the SMU Mustangs moved their games to the Cotton Bowl to accommodate them. The stadium has often been referred to as the "house that Doak built."

In more recent years, the stadium has struggled to retain the same prominence. It is still the site of the Cotton Bowl game and still hosts the annual October clash between the University of Texas and Oklahoma University, a highlight of the State Fair each year. However, it has been eclipsed in recent years by Texas Stadium in

Alabama's Jamie Christenson kicks the game-winning field goal through the uprights in the Crimson Tide's 13–10 victory over Texas Tech in the AT&T Cotton Bowl on January 1, 2006.

Irving, currently the home of the Dallas Cowboys. The Cowboys played their home games at the Cotton Bowl for ten years, from 1960 to 1970. Recently a campaign was mounted to build a new stadium at the site of the Cotton Bowl that would once again house the Cowboys. However, the city leaders were unable to accomplish this task and the Cowboys will be playing in a new stadium in Arlington in 2009. There have also been persistent rumors that the annual battle between Texas and Oklahoma would be moved from the Cotton Bowl in favor of alternating games at the home stadia of both universities. In addition, there has been speculation that the Cotton Bowl game itself would be played in the new Cowboys stadium in Arlington, once that venue is completed. To keep both the Cotton Bowl game and the Texas–Oklahoma game in Fair Park, the State Fair Association and the city of Dallas pledged to fund a $50 million upgrade to increase the stadium's capacity to more than 90,000 seats, making it one of the largest venues for college football in the nation.

The Heart of Big D:
Business, Commerce, and
Government

The Magnolia Building and the Flying Pegasus

January 1, 2000, ushered in the new millennium for the rest of the world, but at precisely midnight on that date, Dallas welcomed a literal beacon from its past. For most of the twentieth century, Pegasus, the flying horse from Greek mythology, could be seen atop the Magnolia

Building in Downtown Dallas. Its glowing red neon silhouette was visible for miles around, a symbol for the city itself. The revolving sign, measuring 30 feet by 50 feet, first made its debut atop the building in 1934 and quickly became an icon for the city. Its image was repro-

Previous page: Detail of Trailing Longhorns *depicting a herd of bronze longhorn steers driven down a grassy hill and into a creek by three bronze cowboys on horseback.*

56

duced not only in the stationery and promotional products of the Magnolia Oil Company but on all manner of advertising items for Dallas in general. By the 1990s, time and weather had taken quite a toll on the sign. In 1997, the city of Dallas, which at the time owned the building, turned the sign off, and for three years the skyline no longer included the familiar red glow of the flying horse. By 1999, the building had new owners and had been reborn as a luxury hotel. A city-wide fundraising drive was mounted to save and restore the sign. Saving the original sign, however, was not possible, as the damage was too great. Instead a $600,000 replica was built and placed atop the building where it still shines. The original sign is now displayed, without neon, in the city's Farmer's Market.

The Magnolia Building was constructed in 1922 to house the headquarters of the Magnolia Oil Company, which went on to become the Mobil Oil Company, now part of Exxon/Mobil, which still calls the Metroplex home. Pegasus was the company's symbol and is still used in some promotional literature today. The 22-story building was designed by architect Alfred C. Bossom and it was mainly known, prior to the flying red horse on its roof, as the tallest building in Texas at the time. Local boosters also pointed out that it was the tallest building south of Washington, D.C., and west of the Mississippi River.

The Adolphus lobby.

Adolphus Hotel

The grande dame of Dallas hotels is the Adolphus, built in 1912 by Adolphus Busch of Budweiser beer fame. Its cost of $2.5 million was a staggering sum at the time, but Busch intended the hotel to be one of the grandest in the Southwest and was willing to pay for it. Dallas city leaders were so enamored of the notion of an elegant hotel being built in its Downtown that they sold Busch the land that City Hall occupied. The stunning Beaux-Arts hotel has undergone numerous additions and renovations.

The architectural firm of the Jerde Partnership of Los Angeles, working with the local firm of Beran and Shelmire, was hired for a major overhaul in 1981 that united all of the additions into a uniform design that reflected the original flavor of the building.

Terraces of the Adolphus.

The Adolphus lobby.

Over the years, the Adolphus has hosted many U.S. presidents, countless foreign dignitaries, and the Queen of England. It was a popular spot in the Swing era for such band leaders as Glenn Miller. In the 1940s, the hotel also gained the distinction of being the first in the United States to be fully air conditioned, not an inconsequential feat given the Texas summer heat. The hotel is located on Commerce Street at Akard, just a few blocks from the flagship store of Nieman-Marcus. Its restaurant, the French Room, is often cited as among the best hotel restaurants in the country.

J. P. Morgan / Chase Tower

Just as the Bank of America Plaza is known locally not by the name of the bank that occupies it but by the distinctive green outline that illuminates it at night, the J. P. Morgan/Chase Tower is known by its most noticeable design feature—from a distance the building appears to have a hole right through its center near its apex. Bank of America Plaza is known as the green building and the Chase Tower is universally referred to as the building with the hole in it. The hole is actually a seven story cutout that begins on the building's 41st floor and extends to the 49th. An observation deck that is serviced by a special elevator is located on the 40th floor and offers a spectacular view of Downtown Dallas.

The Tower anchors the northeast corner of the Arts District. It was completed in 1987, one of the last skyscrapers that emerged in the boom-and-bust decade and was designed by Richard Keating of the firm of Skidmore, Owings, and Merrill. It has 55 stories and is topped by a curved glass half dome. The merger of Bank One and J. P. Morgan/Chase left the combined bank with two signature office buildings in Dallas. The other is Philip Johnson's Bank One Center. In early 2006, J. P. Morgan/Chase announced that it would consolidate its Dallas headquarter operations in the Chase tower and move most of its employees into that building, a move that will no doubt cause yet another Downtown building bearing a prominent bank to change its name.

J. P. Morgan/Chase Tower with Cathedral Santuario de Guadalupe in foreground.

Renaissance Tower

Dallas's modern skyscraper era dates to 1974 when the Renaissance Tower opened. The building is a glass box that is 56 stories tall, located at Elm and Field streets. Only a few buildings were added to the Downtown core during the two decades preceding its construction. When it was completed, Renaissance Tower was the tallest building in Dallas, but that was before the building boom of the early 1980s struck Downtown Dallas and several other taller buildings were constructed.

Originally known as the First International Building, the tower was built by a bank holding company that could trace its roots back to the earliest days of Dallas's banking history.

Being second in any category is not something that Dallasites normally aspire to, but the new owners of Renaissance Tower apparently preferred second place to fifth. When the building was renovated in 2003, several spires were added to the top. This elevated the building's status, making it the second highest in the city.

At the building's base is a one-story glass pyramid containing shops and restaurants. The shops are located below ground, connected to a network of other underground shops and restaurants.

Bank of America Plaza

allas takes pride in its distinction as Big D. In a town where being big and bold is a definite attribute, the designation as the tallest building around is no small claim. At 921 feet and 72 stories, the Bank of America Plaza carries the title of both the tallest building in Dallas and the one that has the most square feet of office space. The building is also a sort of historic artifact of the boom-and-bust 80s. Opened in 1985, the building has borne a succession of names as subsequent bank holding companies merged and failed throughout that decade. Located at 901 Main Street, the building is easily distinguished at night by virtue of the green argon gas tubes that outline the entire building creating a very impressive and distinctive silhouette. The view of the building is particularly striking from the gardens of the nearby Nasher Sculpture Center.

Like many other building projects planned in the 1980s, this one was conceived as a complex of buildings that would have been equally spectacular. There were to be four buildings in all; one would have been outlined with purple argon tubing as a counterpoint to the green of this one.

Venture, *a large bright red sculpture outside the Bank of America Plaza, by Russian-American sculptor Alexander Liberman, created with Cor-Ten steel.*

Bank One Center

Few major American architects have gained as much through high-profile commissions in the Dallas/Fort Worth Metroplex as Philip Johnson. He has designed museums, office buildings, and memorials over almost three decades. His buildings in the area have run the gamut from towering skyscrapers to urban gardens that offer a welcome relief from the hustle and bustle of the city centers. In 1961, his first major Metroplex commission, the Amon Carter Museum, opened in Fort Worth, followed a few years later by the Downtown Fort Worth Water Gardens. He was chosen to design the John F. Kennedy Memorial in Dealey Plaza by Stanley Marcus, and later to design Thanksgiving Square. His 60-story office building at 1717 Main Street in Dallas, first known as Momentum Center and then as Bank One Center, was completed in 1987 when he was 81. It is the third-tallest building in Dallas. The building is designed as a series of barrel vaults that are positioned at right angles from one another at varying heights.

Below the building lies one of Dallas's least-known Downtown features, a system of pedestrian tunnels that link many of the city's office buildings. Workers roam through a large system of retail shops and restaurants, all protected from the extremes of winter and summer temperatures.

Thanksgiving Square

In 1907, a very unusual event occurred in Dallas. Led by Rabbi William Greenburg, who had arrived only a short time before to take the helm of Temple Emanu-El, the oldest Jewish congregation in the city, Dallas religious leaders called for a citywide celebration and commemoration of Thanksgiving. Protestants, Catholics, and Jews responded to the invitation and gathered in Downtown Dallas for a Thanksgiving Day service that featured speeches by leaders from several area churches. That service started a tradition that lasted for the next fifty years and also served as the inspiration behind Dallas businessman Peter Stewart's idea to form a monument to the idea of world Thanksgiving. Stewart founded the Thanksgiving Foundation, lobbied city leaders to consider designating land in Downtown Dallas for a Thanksgiving memorial, and spearheaded fundraising efforts to construct the memorial.

Land was acquired in the heart of Downtown Dallas in 1968 at the intersection of Pacific, Bryan, and Ervay streets. Noted architect Philip Johnson, who only recently had created a unique Downtown park in Fort Worth, the Water Gardens, was commissioned to create an appropriate memorial to Thanksgiving and a meditation area. Johnson designed a white marble spiral chapel amidst a quiet oasis of green space and water elements that offer a spot for quiet reflec-

tion in the middle of an urban landscape. It opened in 1976 on the 200th anniversary of Thanksgiving in America.

In the thirty years since the Square was dedicated, the foundation has worked to carry the message of Thanksgiving to the world.

Farmer's Market

The rich black land prairie around Dallas was one of the original reasons for the city's creation. Cotton dominated much of the farming in the surrounding area and quickly established Dallas as one of the leading centers for its production and shipping. However, farmers have always cultivated much of the land

around Dallas for fruits and vegetables. Almost from the city's inception, farmers came to town to sell produce, as well as livestock. In 1941, the very informal arrangement whereby farmers assembled at a makeshift marketplace just south of the central city became somewhat more official with the construction of the first permanent structure for the Farmer's Market. Other buildings have been added over the years and present plans by the city of Dallas call for a major expansion to take place in the near future.

Today, many modern growers, along with produce wholesalers, offer a bounty of fresh produce directly to customers at the Dallas Farmer's Market, which is located at 1010 South Pearl, near Downtown. These sellers continue a tradition of selling directly to customers that started in virtually the same location in the nineteenth century.

The market is housed in four long open-air pavilions and is open daily from 7 a.m. to 6 p.m. In addition to fruits and vegetables, vendors also offer flowers, garden supplies, and a variety of handcrafted items. Several special events are held at the market throughout the year as well as cooking classes conducted by some of Dallas's most prominent chefs.

The Crescent

In 1985, the Rosewood Corporation opened the Crescent Court, a complex of three 18-story office buildings surrounding an upscale luxury hotel just north of the Downtown financial district. At the time, the development designed by the architectural firm of Philip Johnson and John Burgee seemed a little out of place, a little out of scale to the neighborhood, and certainly a departure from the other buildings that Johnson and Burgee had created in the Dallas/Fort Worth area. The whole complex has a deliberate European feel that some observers have labeled as "over the top." Twenty years later, the Crescent has become one of the anchors of the Uptown development that has spread northward from Downtown and transformed the area into a hip and decidedly young residential and entertainment district.

The Crescent has remained true to its upscale roots and remains one of the premier hotel and office complexes in Texas. On occasion the royal family of Saudia Arabia has been known to reserve entire floors of the hotel. Rosewood also owns the nearby Mansion on Turtle Creek, a smaller boutique hotel, whose clientele is of the same caliber. On the other hand, Uptown is an eclectic mix of shops, restaurants, and clubs that stretches along either side of McKinney Avenue northward toward the exclusive twin cities of Highland Park and University Park. The Crescent is located on its southern edge near the increasingly active Arts District.

Reunion Tower

For several decades, the most noticeable element of the Dallas skyline was the flying red Pegasus on top of the Magnolia Building. However, as more tall buildings began to dominate Dallas's Downtown, the Pegasus became harder to see from a distance. As a symbol and icon of Dallas, the flying horse was supplanted in the late 1970s by a new architectural feature in the night sky, the revolving sphere on top of Reunion Tower. This addition is part of a complex developed in a formerly blighted area at the southwestern edge of Downtown and built by oilman and philanthropist Ray Hunt. The complex also includes Reunion Arena and the Hyatt hotel. The sphere is a brightly lit, geodesic dome 560 feet tall sitting on four cylinders. It contains an observation deck at the 52nd floor and a restaurant that revolves completely every 55 minutes, offering a truly panoramic 360-degree view of Dallas and the surrounding area. Reunion Arena served as the home to the Dallas Mavericks prior to the construction of American Airlines Center a few miles to the north. In the aftermath of Hurricane Katrina, the arena served as a shelter for families displaced from New Orleans.

The tower and arena are named after one of the most interesting experiments in Dallas's early history, a utopian settlement begun by French socialists in the early 1850s called La Reunion. Around 200 French, Swiss, and Belgian settlers joined the colony on land in present-day Oak Cliff that had been purchased from the original Peters Colony. At one point the Peters Colony controlled all the land that Dallas and Fort Worth now occupy. Due to poor financial management, La Reunion disbanded by the mid 1850s; however, it left a lasting imprint on the area. Most of the other settlers in the Dallas area were farmers; while, most of the La Reunion colonists were artisans, tradesmen, craftsmen, even artists and musicians. Many stayed in the area and added their many talents to the fledgling settlement. Ironically, their lack of farming experience probably contributed greatly to the failure of the colony, but their many other skills gave Dallas a tremendous boost in its development as a new city.

Fountain Place

It is no secret that Texas summers can be real scorchers; in 1980, the high temperature in Dallas climbed above 100 degrees Fahrenheit for 40 consecutive days. Now as then, the temperature on a July evening can still be upward of 90 degrees even at 10 p.m. No wonder, then, that a tree-shaded water garden complete with 200 computer-synchronized water jets would be a favorite spot for visitors and residents alike on a typical summer day. Fountain Place, located in the Arts District at 1445 Ross Avenue, offers welcome relief with its splashing fountains and 200 cypress trees arranged on a 5.8-acre plaza beneath what some have called Dallas's best-designed office tower.

The building was completed in 1986 and designed by Henry Cobb of the I. M. Pei studio. It is one of six projects the Pei studio completed in Dallas, all in the 1980s before the crash in the oil and real estate markets brought Downtown Dallas development to a screeching halt. Cobb has described his emerald green glass skyscraper as "what's left after carving into a square prism." Indeed the carved prism effect makes the building appear quite differently according to what vantage point the viewer is looking from.

Originally, the building was designed to be one of two identical buildings that would face one another. The second building was never completed, leaving Fountain Place to dominate the northwestern corner of Downtown Dallas alone.

Dallas City Hall

One of the most architecturally significant buildings in Dallas is City Hall, located on the southern edge of Downtown near the Convention Center. Designed by I. M. Pei, and one of six projects his firm has developed for Dallas, the building was completed in 1978 at a cost of around $43 million. It is the fifth structure to serve Dallas as City Hall; the earlier four were not particularly known for their architectural merits. The fourth one, still used today for some governmental operations, was primarily famous as the site where Lee Harvey Oswald, the alleged assassin of President John F. Kennedy, was shot by Jack Ruby as he was being transferred to a county facility.

Some people have argued that city fathers wanted to break free of the stigma of that event by commissioning a truly world-class facility for City Hall, one that would show Dallas as a modern and forward-looking metropolitan area. Pei certainly delivered on that notion with his dramatically cantilevered seven-story building that appears to be on the verge of tipping over. Each floor is significantly wider than the one immediately below it, giving the illusion of a triangle balanced on its edge. Modern sculptures, including Henry Moore's *Dallas Piece*, and a small lake grace the exterior grounds.

Although the building is now nearly thirty years old, its startling design still attracts photographers and architectural students from around the world.

The Wilson Building

As in many other cities, the Downtown core of Dallas went through a slow decline in the 1960s and 1970s with little new construction and even less historic renovation and restoration. While the 1980s saw a boom in office building construction with several leading architects creating distinctive new steel and glass towers, most activity in Downtown Dallas ceased with the end of the workday. Weekends found few people wandering among those newly constructed towers. Thousands of people worked Downtown, but very few lived there; consequently the city's center lacked vitality and energy.

Gradually development has returned to the Downtown sector, led by the construction of new office towers, cultural facilities, and a few high-rise condominium projects. In recent years a new grocery store has opened in a restored office building in anticipation of a growing number of new residents to the Downtown area. Some of Dallas's most venerable buildings from the early twentieth century are finding new life as apartment and condominium complexes. The Wilson Building, located at Elm, Ervay, and Main streets across the street from Neiman-Marcus, was one of the first historic buildings to be part of this Downtown revitalization. Built in 1903 and modeled after the Grand Opera House in Paris, the Wilson Building housed the Titche-Goettinger Department store, one of the city's first such establishments. The building was built by local businessman John B. Wilson and designed by the prestigious Fort Worth architecture firm of Sanguinett and Statts. The building was tall by 1903 standards with eight stories and one of the city's most elegant in terms of design. Today it is the home of loft apartments whose residents once again bring life to Dallas's Downtown canyons, even after 5 p.m.

Detail of Trailing Longhorns *sculpture.*

Trailing Longhorns Sculpture in Pioneer Plaza Park

Nearby to two of Dallas's most contemporary examples of architecture and sculpture, I. M. Pei's City Hall and Henry Moore's abstract sculpture *The Dallas Piece*, is another work of art that evokes an entirely different era and aesthetic. Robert Summers' *Trailing Longhorns* in Pioneer Plaza Park depicts 40 larger-than-life longhorn steers driven by three cowboys (one African-American, one Hispanic, and one Anglo) across a landscape of rolling hills, trees, and a stream. Summers actually created the landscape design as well as the figures. Originally the piece was to have been almost twice its present size with the addition of 30 more steers. As it is, *Trailing Longhorns* is said to be the world's largest bronze sculpture (if one considers the entirety of the piece as opposed to looking at it as 43 separate sculptures).

The piece, along with the plaza, was commissioned by the Texas Trees Foundation with strong support from developer Trammell Crow. It did not receive unanimous acclaim at its dedication, with some critics from the local art community decrying the piece as irrelevant to the history and heritage of Dallas. Those critics claimed that Fort Worth, with its well-documented connection to the early Texas cattle industry, would have been a more appropriate location. The sculpture's supporters have countered that an early cattle drive route ran not far from where the piece is located. Whatever the case may be (and there is historical evidence for both arguments), no one can deny that the sculpture is one of the most visited sites in Dallas and may well be the most frequently photographed sculpture in all of Texas.

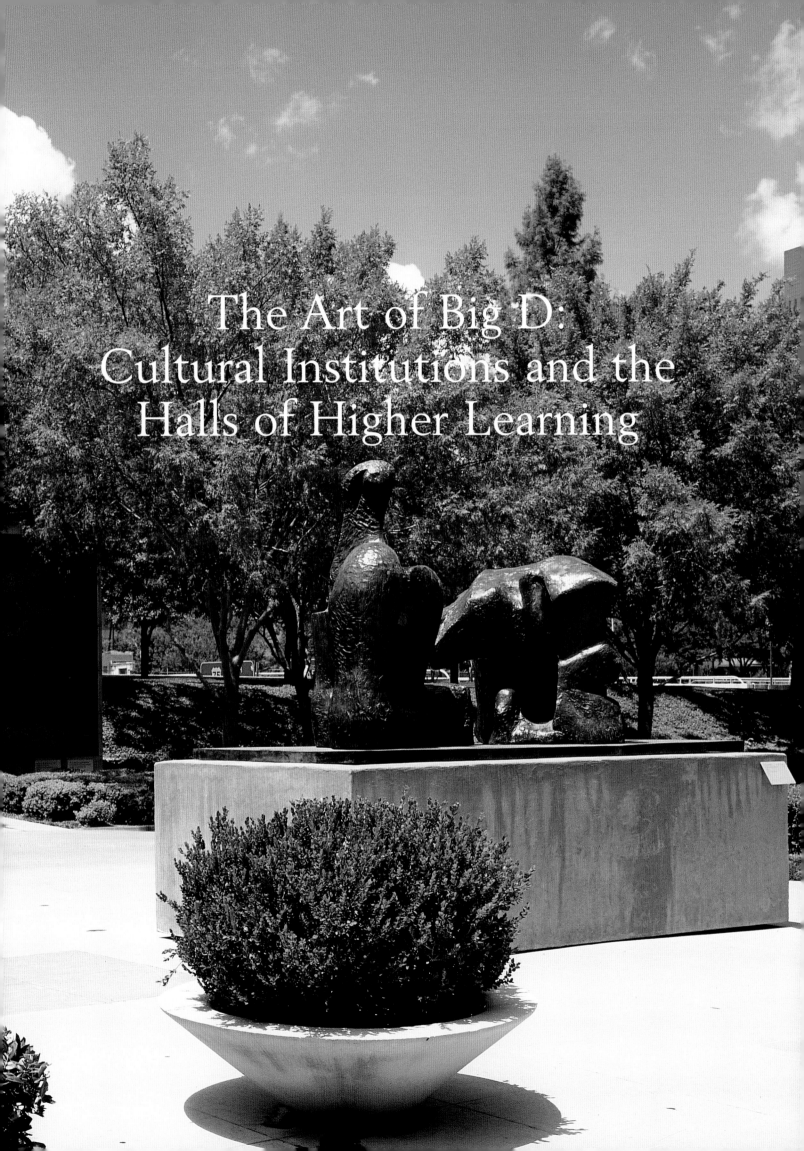

The Art of Big D:
Cultural Institutions and the
Halls of Higher Learning

Dallas Museum of Art

Anchoring the Dallas Arts District, the largest urban Arts District in the nation, is the Dallas Museum of Art, an art museum with over 23,000 works that extend over 5,000 years of art history. The museum has extensive collections in the fields of American and European fine art, pre-Colombian antiquities, and decorative arts. In recent years, it has also embarked on an aggressive expansion of its contemporary art collection.

The present structure, designed by architect Edward Barnes, opened in 1984 and was financed by a combination of city bond money and private donations. The limestone building is dominated by a central barrel vault. In 1993, the Nancy and Jake Hamon Building opened, displaying a permanent exhibition of the art of the Americas. Also designed by Barnes, the Hamon Building added 140,000 square feet to the original 210,000-square-foot structure. The museum organizes and hosts major exhibitions on a wide variety of themes each year. It also offers a diverse array of educational programming that ranges from readings of stories by Texas authors to musical performances and more traditional art history lectures.

Previous page: Dallas Museum of Art.

The museum began as the Dallas Art Association in 1903 when a group of citizens organized exhibitions at the city's original Carnegie Library building. After switching locations several times, the museum moved to a building of its own in Fair Park and changed its name to the Dallas Museum of Fine Arts in 1934. After that building was extensively damaged by a hailstorm, the museum moved into a new building constructed as part of the Texas Centennial Exposition celebration held in Fair Park in 1936. It remained there until 1984.

The museum's collections, programs, and buildings have steadily grown since its move to the Arts District. It is the only comprehensive art museum in North Texas and ranks among the largest city art museums in the country.

Nasher Sculpture Center

Of all the facilities in the Arts District, the building that has received the most acclaim is at first glance the simplest, the elegant Nasher Sculpture Center. Renzo Piano's design for the Center effectively achieved founding collector Raymond Nasher's vision for an "outdoor garden and roofless museum" to house his exceptional collection of modern sculpture assembled over a 50-year period by Nasher and his wife, Patsy. Piano created five long galleries that invite visitors into the museum from the street, through the building to the exquisitely designed sculpture garden at the other end of the gallery. The building actually does have a roof, but one that utilizes an innovative system that filters natural light continually into the galleries.

Piano's building makes the transition from inside to outside a seamless experience; visitors can move between the two spaces easily and naturally. Outside in the garden, both very large and more human scale sculptures are arranged on a rectangular field of grass and trees. At its end are another rectangle, a reflecting pool, and James Turrell's *Tending (Blue)*, a piece the artist describes as a skyplace. It was specifically designed for this particular spot and consists of a room with an open ceiling. Lights of different colors are carefully orchestrated to work with the natural cycles of night and day.

Nasher, who is the developer of the NorthPark shopping center, first shared his collection with the public by placing a rotating selection of sculptures at the shopping center. He then developed an extensive traveling exhibition that toured museums both in this country and abroad. He was courted by such major museums as the Guggenheim in New York, the National Gallery in Washington, D.C., and the Museum of Fine Arts in Boston, with offers of permanent gallery spaces if he were to give the collection or a substantial portion to the museums. The city of Dallas offered to build a new museum to house the collection, but Nasher chose instead to fund the museum himself in order to control the quality of the project. The result is the breathtaking museum that opened across the street from the Dallas Museum of Art in 2003.

Opposite and below: Bodies Past and Present, *the* Figurative Tradition *in the Nasher Collection.*

Suspended in light, the skybridge inside the Crow Collection of Asian Art bridges artwork from China and India spanning two galleries, and is supported by a first-floor gallery designated to the arts of Japan.

Trammell and Margaret Crow Collection of Asian Art

Dallas real estate developer Trammell Crow and his wife Margaret first traveled to China in 1976, only a short time after Americans first received permission to visit the communist regime. Crow had created the Dallas Trade Center and was invited to China to attend the

Canton Trade Fair. Over the years and through many trips to China and Asia, the Crows developed a keen taste and an educated eye for a wide cross-section of Eastern art.

Eventually their collection grew to over 7,000 items spread across many time periods and cultures and included art from China, India, Japan, and Southeast Asia. Around 700 of the finest examples of their collection are now housed in elegant galleries in a Downtown skyscraper located across the street from the Nasher Sculpture Center in the heart of Downtown Dallas. The museum is housed in three galleries on the lower levels of the building and was conceived both as a legacy for the Crows' children and grandchildren and as a gift to the citizens of Dallas. Among the highlights of the collection is an extensive collection of jade that is said to be among the finest in the country.

Several selections from the Crow collection are shared each year in traveling exhibitions that tour throughout the United States. In addition, the Crow Collection hosts a number of special exhibitions each year, some developed from its permanent collection and some developed by other institutions. All displays are open to the public at no admission charge.

In recent years, the Crows have turned over management of the collection and its supporting foundation to their son, Trammell S. Crow, who has continued the collecting tradition of his parents.

An exquisite look into the Indian Gallery inside the Crow Collection of Asian Art.

Morton H. Meyerson Symphony Center

The new Dallas Museum of Art was the first cultural facility in Dallas's urban Arts District; the Morton H. Meyerson Symphony Center was the second. Both buildings were products of a public/private fundraising formula that has proved a successful method of building world-class facilities in Downtown Dallas. Both buildings are owned by the city of Dallas, but managed by private organizations. Like the art museum, the Symphony Center was designed by a nationally acclaimed architect, in this case I. M. Pei, who had already designed the Dallas City Hall as well as other Downtown buildings. The Center opened in 1989 and is home to the Dallas Symphony Orchestra as well as other performing arts groups. The building is noted not only for its striking design, but also for its outstanding acoustics. When the facility was planned, symphony leaders decided to match the

The Lay Family Organ is one of the hallmarks of The Morton H. Meyerson Symphony Center.

quality of the architectural design with the quality of the acoustic design and hired acoustician Russell Johnson to work hand in hand with Pei throughout the design and construction phases.

The largest private grant made to the project was a $10 million gift by Ross Perot, founder of Electronic Data Systems. Perot was given the opportunity to name the facility and rather than choosing his own name or that of a family member, he decided instead to honor his long-time friend and business associate, Morton H. Meyerson, who had long been a Dallas civic leader. One of the hallmarks of the Center is the massive Lay Family Organ which plays through 4,535 pipes. The Meyerson is located at the eastern end of the Arts District.

Cathedral Santuario de Guadalupe

Although its cornerstone was laid in 1898 and the building held services as early as 1902, architect Nicholas Clayton's original vision for the Dallas Diocese (established in 1890) was not actually realized until 2005, when a multimillion-dollar capital campaign culminated with the dedication of a twenty-story tower that holds a 49-bell carillon.

The oldest building in the Dallas Arts District, the Cathedral Santuario de Guadalupe, now stands as a testament to the talents of one of Texas's most renowned architects of the nineteenth century. Many of its neighbors are examples of the work some of the most renowned architects of the twentieth century, including Edward Barnes, I. M. Pei, and Renzo Piano.

The church was originally named Sacred Heart Cathedral and at its inception was located in a largely residential neighborhood. Now it is surrounded by skyscrapers, art museums, and the Dallas Center for the Performing Arts (a complex of several buildings). Its congregation has also changed dramatically over the years and is now largely Hispanic. It boasts the second-largest congregation in the country with approximately 50,000 members.

Located at 2215 Ross Avenue at Pearl Street, the cathedral's original design was not completed in 1902 due to a lack of funds. Although Clayton died in 1916 long before his original design was completed, both his grandson and great grandson were present at the dedication ceremony.

Latino Cultural Center

In the spring of 2006, 500,000 Latinos marched through the streets of Dallas to protest proposed congressional legislation on immigration reform. While many other cities across the country also saw demonstrations, the one in Dallas was among the largest and most well organized. If anyone doubted that Dallas had become a center for Latinos in the United States, this show of solidarity should have dispelled that notion.

Latino students form the majority population in the Dallas Independent School District and Latinos, already the largest minority population, will soon be the majority population in the city. Given this dramatic demographic shift, it is appropriate that one of the most recent cultural institutions to be built in Dallas is the Latino Cultural Center, which was created through a public/private partnership utilizing city bond money and private donations. The dramatic and colorful center was designed by renowned Mexican architect Ricardo Legorreta and includes a 300-seat theater, along with art and sculpture galleries.

The center is operated by the city of Dallas through its Office of Cultural Affairs. Its mission is "to provide artists, cultural organizations, and the Latino community with the facilities and opportunities to develop and celebrate unique cultural talents and gifts."

Each year the center hosts art exhibitions, often featuring the work of local Latino artists, dramatic performances, dance performances, and many other presentations that highlight the diversity and creativity of the city's vibrant Latino population.

Texas Woman's University

Texas Woman's University was founded in Denton in 1901 and has undergone several name changes in the last 100 years reflecting its growth and evolution. The university, despite its name, has admitted men since 1972, but its student population is still primarily female. It has a strong tradition in the visual arts, including photography. Carlotta Copran, whose entire body of work is now in the permanent collection of the Amon Carter Museum in Fort Worth, was a longtime faculty member there.

In addition to fine arts, the school is particularly strong in its programs for health care providers. It also attracts many students to its library sciences program. The university carries the distinction of the being the largest state-supported school primarily for women.

One of the university's most notable resources is the Woman's Collection at the library. The collection is an historical archive that numbers over 40,000 books, 3,000 manuscripts, and 19,000 photographs all relating to women. The collection, which is still actively growing, was originally developed to inspire women students.

University of Dallas

ocated in the Las Colinas section of Irving and close to Texas Stadium (although both the university and the Cowboys bear the Dallas name, neither are actually located within the city), the University of Dallas is a small, but academically challenging, Roman Catholic institution. The university was founded in 1956 and now serves around 3,500 students. It does, however, boast the largest Master of Business Administration program in the Metroplex, larger even than that of Southern Methodist University.

The campus is spread over 225 acres tucked in between two major highways. Part of the campus, including a graceful central tower, was designed by noted native Texas architect O'Neil Ford, who also designed several homes in the area as well as the campus of Trinity University in San Antonio; both campuses share many design similarities. Although relatively small in terms of student population, the university surprised many area observers by mounting an aggressive and well-regarded plan to land the George W. Bush Presidential Library in 2005. The university offered the library a prominent location overlooking the city of Dallas and managed to make the final cut with four other larger universities.

Texas Christian University

Texas Christian University (TCU), long associated with Fort Worth, where it has been located since 1910, actually did not move there until over forty years after its founding.

That was not the original plan by brothers Addison and Randolph Clark. Their original intention was to locate a new co-educational college, one of the first such institutions in the Southwest, in Fort Worth shortly after the U.S. Civil War. The brothers were devout Christians (the college is affiliated with, but not governed by, the Christian Church/Disciples of Christ) and had actually procured land in Fort Worth to establish the college. Their plans changed though with the advent of the cattle trade in 1870s. The area of the city that the college was planned for gradually became known for its saloons and brothels catering to the increasing number of rowdy cowboys who came to town to let off steam after or during long cattle drives. The brothers Clark simply felt that Fort Worth was not an appropriate place to found a Christian college. Instead they first started the school in a small community forty miles to the southwest of Fort Worth in 1873 and eventually moved the university to Waco, already home to Baylor, a Baptist University, in 1895. After that campus burned, the brothers were persuaded to return to Fort Worth through a gift of 50 acres on the city's West Side, still the site of the campus, and $200,000 in cash. Apparently, by 1910 Fort Worth had been properly rehabilitated.

Originally the school was known as the

The Robert Carr Chapel, erected in 1953. The building is designed in a Georgian Colonial Revival style, the spire is intentionally the highest point on campus, and the chapel itself is one of TCU's favorite and most well-known landmarks.

AddRan Male and Female College, named after its founders. Today with an endowment topping $1 billion, the school has nearly 9,000 students who are enrolled in nine schools. The College of Humanities and Social Sciences retains the original AddRan name and has recently instituted a Center for Texas Studies. Among TCU's notable graduates is CBS newsman Bob Schieffer, for whom the School of Journalism is named.

University of North Texas

The largest university in the Dallas/Fort Worth area is located thirty miles to the north in Denton. The 32,000 students who now attend the school make it the fourth largest in Texas. In the near future, the university will be even larger with the establishment of a separate campus in South Dallas, the first university to be located in that part of Dallas County.

The Dallas campus is part of an ambitious master plan that includes offering classes at a facility in Downtown Dallas. The school also operates the University of North Texas Health Science Center in the Cultural District in Fort Worth.

The university started rather modestly on the second floor of a hardware store in the Denton town square in 1890. It was then known as the Texas Normal School and Teacher Training Institute. Since then it has undergone several name changes, the latest from North Texas State University to the University of North Texas. Although active in many different academic areas, the university is perhaps best known for its jazz and music program that attracts students from all over the world, and is extremely competitive in terms of its stature with other universities.

Recently the university began an extensive digitization project known as the Portal to Texas History that will make archival material from several Texas historical organizations and libraries available online.

Meadows Museum with Santiago Calatrava's Wave *(2002) in foreground.*

Southern Methodist University / Meadows Museum

In the early years of the twentieth century, the United Methodist Church was searching for an appropriate site to build a new university in the southern United States. Several cities were considered, but citizens in Dallas pledged to raise $300,000 in 1911 to help establish the new school if the Methodists chose their city. By 1915, the university's first building was open and ready for business. It sat on a hilltop north of the city. As a tribute to the generosity that made it possible, the new university, which was named Southern Methodist University (SMU), named the building Dallas Hall. Today the first building is still one of its most prominent.

Throughout its history, the school has continued to prosper through the generous donations of area residents, including Algur Meadows, whose name is on both the School of Art and a world-class art museum on the campus. The latter contains the largest collection of Spanish art outside of Spain. The Meadows Foundation, one of the largest in Texas, recently made a gift of $33 million to the university to support exhibitions and educational programs at the museum.

Eleven thousand students now attend the university, which offers degrees in various academic schools. SMU is located in the town of University Park, one of the area's most affluent suburbs. Originally the town grew up around the university as a place where its professors and students could live. In those days, the university had more land than buildings, certainly not the case today. In recent years, its president, Dr. Gerald Turner, has said, "In the early days we sold land by the acre, now we are buying it back by the square foot." The university has not been without its share of both glory and controversy, particularly in the area of sports. One of its most celebrated football stars was Doak Walker, who was so popular that the university moved its home games to the Cotton Bowl (see page 52) to accommodate more fans. For many years that facility was known as the "house that Doak built." On the other hand, the NCAA issued its one and only "death penalty" to the school in the 1980s, suspending football operations due to recurring violations involving athletes and team boosters. Although the football program has been reinstated, it has yet to achieve its former status.

SMU is a private university of 11,000 students in the vibrant heart of Dallas. This academic community values small classes, hands-on research, and programs that expand students' experiences beyond the classroom.

At Ease in the Metroplex:
Sporting and Shopping
Venues

There is no bigger sport in Texas than football and no bigger team in terms of its fan base, economic value, and mystique than the Dallas Cowboys, winner of five Super Bowls.

Since 1971, the team has played its home games not in Dallas, but in nearby Irving, at Texas Stadium, the 65,000-seat venue that is known by the signature hole in its roof. In the early 1970s when the team was owned by Dallas oilman Clint Murchison and managed by Tex Schramm, it became known as "America's Team," one of the most successful public relations ploys ever developed by an American sports franchise. Shortly after the team moved from its original home at the Cotton Bowl in Dallas's Fair Park, local sportswriters joked that the hole in the stadium allowed "God to see America's team play."

America's Team began as an expansion franchise in 1959 and its early years were a struggle. The Cowboys shared the Cotton Bowl with another start-up team, the Dallas Texans of the new American Football League, owned by Lamar Hunt. Murchison and Hunt agreed that Dallas was only big enough for one professional team, and Hunt packed his team farther north where they became the Kansas City Chiefs.

The Cowboys played in the Cotton Bowl throughout the 1960s and gradually developed under the tutelage of head coach Tom Landry into one of the league's better teams. In 1967, they nearly brought a championship home to the Cotton Bowl only to be defeated at the hands of the Green Bay Packers. The following year, they lost another close one to the Packers, this time on the Packers' home field, in the famous Ice Bowl. The Packers went on to play the Kansas City Chiefs in the first Super Bowl.

By the time the Cowboys departed Fair Park for the brand new Texas Stadium in 1971, they had captured the imagination of much of the country. The Cowboys won Super Bowls in the

1970s, but went into a competitive decline in the 1980s, as did the fortune of their owner, Clint Murchison. Like many others in Dallas, he was caught in the oil and real estate bust of that decade and was forced to sell the team. His original $600,000 investment netted him $80 million when he sold the team. The Cowboys were sold again to their present owner, Jerry

Previous page: Texas Motor Speedway.

Jones, in 1989, this time for $140 million. Now, three more Super Bowl wins later, the team is valued at nearly $800 million.

In 2009, the Dallas Cowboys, who have not actually played in Dallas for over 35 years, will move to another Metroplex city, Arlington, which is located midway between Dallas and Fort Worth into a new state-of-the-art stadium with a retractable roof. They may no longer be America's Team, but the Cowboys are still the biggest game in town as far as the Metroplex is concerned.

Team introduction of the Dallas Cowboys during the Dallas Cowboys 31–28 win over the Kansas City Chiefs at Texas Stadium in Irving, Texas, December 2005.

Ameriquest Field in Arlington. Shot on Opening Day, April 3, 2006. Texas Rangers against the Boston Red Sox. This particular photo was shot during the singing of the national anthem, sung by country music great Charley Pride.

Ameriquest Field

Dallas and Fort Worth have been home to professional baseball since the birth of the Texas League in 1888. Both cities sported several different teams throughout the first fifty years of the twentieth century, most notably the Dallas Steers and the Fort Worth Cats, both of which competed in the Texas League. On two occasions, teams in Fort Worth and Dallas were combined to form one franchise with the teams splitting their home games between the two cities. Finally, in 1972 the minor league era of Dallas/Fort Worth baseball ended when the major leagues came to the area in the form of the Washington Senators, who moved from the nation's capital to Arlington, Texas, to become the Texas Rangers.

The Rangers have been playing adjacent to Six Flags Over Texas just south of Interstate 30 for 34 years with a fairly consistent fan base, but little success in postseason play. The team's original stadium, simply named Arlington Stadium, was torn down to make way for a new one designed by David Schwarz which opened in 1994. Originally called the Ball Park in Arlington, the stadium's name was changed to Ameriquest Field after the home mortgage company bought the naming rights for $75 million spread over a 30-year period. The new red-brick stadium has a decidedly urban retro feel in a suburban setting.

American Airlines Center

Washington, D.C., architect David Schwarz has made a big impact on the Dallas/Fort Worth Metroplex. He has designed museums, performance halls, town halls, even whole neighborhood shopping centers. However, he may be best known for his contribution to the area's most prominent new sporting venues. He designed both the home for the Texas Rangers major league baseball team in Arlington and a newer stadium for the minor league Frisco Rough Riders in the northern suburbs of Dallas.

Much closer to the heart of Dallas is the American Airlines Center, which is located near the city's original settlement. The massive red-brick arena Schwarz designed is home to the Dallas Mavericks of the National Basketball Association and the Dallas Stars of the National Hockey League. In addition to the home games of those two teams, the arena is the site of concerts and such traveling extravaganzas as the Ringling Brothers Circus.

The American Airlines Center anchors one of the city's newest and most ambitious urban developments known simply as Victory. The arena, along with such upscale hotels as the W, high-rise condominiums, and several thousand square feet of retail and entertainment venues, was built on a once-blighted area just north of the historic West End warehouse district. Its developers have touted the emerging neighborhood as a new model for modern urban living with working, shopping, and living spaces built within walking distance of one another and with easy access to DART, Dallas's mass transit system.

Dallas Mavericks fan whooping it up.

Lone Star Park

Horse racing has long been a favorite pastime in the Dallas area, dating back to the very early days of the State Fair. For a brief period in the early 1930s, pari-mutuel betting was legalized by the Texas legislature, and Arlington Downs racetrack, located approximately 15 miles east of Dallas, was one of the state's most popular racing venues. The legislature reversed itself in 1937, making betting illegal for the next 50 years. In 1987, betting once again became

legal, and new facilities gradually began to appear throughout the state. Lone Star Park opened ten years later with a one-mile dirt oval and a ⅞-mile turf track. The facility was built in the city of Grand Prairie only a short distance from where Arlington Downs had stood.

Racing fans who have also attended baseball games at the nearby Ameriquest Field or hockey or basketball games at American Airlines Center in Dallas may notice some design familiarity in all three venues; each one was a product of the David Schwarz architectural studio. The facility sits on 315 acres and features a seven-story grandstand with both outdoor and indoor seating and dining facilities. There are two racing seasons; thoroughbreds compete in the spring and summer and quarter horses race in the fall.

North Park Shopping Center

eveloper Ray Nasher has always been a visionary. For one thing, in the early 1960s he envisioned that a former cotton field at the intersection of U.S. Highway 75 (Central Expressway) and Loop 12 (Northwest Highway) would be in the not-too-distant future a central location for a new shopping experience. As it was, when he first surveyed the area, the available land appeared to be far north and quite distant from the retail center of Downtown Dallas. Nasher accurately predicted the inexorable movement of Dallas residents northward toward new suburbs and also that these residents would increasingly prefer to shop much closer to home.

Location was one thing, but Nasher's genius also lay in his aesthetic vision for NorthPark Center. Although it is far larger today than it was when it opened in 1965 (a 2005 addition brought the total number of stores to 200 and made it one of the largest shopping malls in Texas), NorthPark still has the same atmosphere of serenity, beauty, and simplicity—attributes not normally associated with a mega-shopping complex, particularly one that typically serves over 200,000 shoppers per weekend. The center's polished concrete floors and easily navigable open spaces also supply the perfect stage for selections from Nasher's extensive and acclaimed collection of contemporary sculpture. Long before the Nasher Sculpture Center was opened, shoppers were treated to many of the pieces that are currently on display at that Downtown location. In addition to mounting his own collection, Nasher has always envisioned NorthPark as a place for art as well as commerce. The center frequently plays host to exhibits and displays of other art forms.

The monumental Ad Astra, 2005, *a 48-foot-tall, 12-ton, giant, orange steel sculpture by internationally renowned New York artist Mark di Suvero takes center stage in the new NorthCourt.* Ad Astra *is owned by Nancy A. Nasher and David J. Haemisegger.*

Snider Plaza / University Park

In an era when shopping centers are increasingly homogenous and dominated by the same national chains, Snider Plaza, located off Hillcrest Avenue near Southern Methodist University in University Park, is decidedly eclectic. Unlike Highland Park Village, which was developed and designed around a unifying central aesthetic, Snider Plaza embraces a number of styles and types of buildings.

Part of its appeal no doubt owes much to its proximity to the university, which has steadily grown since its inception in 1915. The town of University Park, where both the plaza and university are located, grew up around the school initially as a place where the professors and students could live.

The four-block area of Snider Plaza, with over 80 unique shops and restaurants, celebrates the fact that all of its tenants lean more toward the unique rather than the "cookie-cutter" styles of national chains.

A wide variety of mostly locally owned restaurants are available in the plaza, including such longtime mainstays as Kuby's Delicatessen and Peggy Sue's Barbecue. The plaza has been around since 1927, when Wichita Falls businessman C. W. Snider bought the land for around 80 cents an acre. Snider put in the central fountain almost immediately, but the rest of the buildings were added gradually over the next several years due to the economic downturn of the Depression.

Texas Motor Speedway

With three major racing weekends, two from motor racing's most popular series, NASCAR, and one from the Indy Racing League (open-wheeled cars), and a large number of other special events throughout the year, the Texas Motor Speedway hosts over a million race fans each year. Opened in 1997, the Speedway was the first NASCAR track in Texas, and continues to be one of the most popular sporting venues in the South. Located a few miles west of Interstate 35 and twenty miles north of Fort Worth, the Texas Motor Speedway is a mammoth facility that can accommodate 150,000 fans around its 1.5-mile steeply banked oval track. Race weekends create an almost self-contained culture with thousands of fans camping in motor homes or in tents adjacent to the track. Many arrive for qualifying laps on the Thursday preceding the races and stay for the entire weekend. The NASCAR events feature three separate races, while the Indy weekend usually has two events.

A few race fans need not leave the speedway at all if they have purchased one of the luxury condominiums that overlook the second turn. A nearby high-rise hotel is available for those who prefer a more traditional place to spend the night during race weekends. An eighteen-hole golf course is available across the highway.

Stonebriar Centre Mall / Frisco

More than a few Dallas observers and historians have noted with some surprise that the growth in the area has marched northward at a far greater rate than to the south, where the landscape is much more varied. Perhaps the Trinity River has been a psychological barrier as well as a physical one. Dallas was founded where it was precisely because that was the area that allowed for the easiest crossing of the river. North/south and east/west Indian trails crossed at that spot above the river and later the Republic of Texas commissioned a road roughly along the same north/south route. The road became Preston Road, which is still a major thoroughfare leading from near Downtown through the early suburbs of Highland Park and University Park and now through Plano and even more suburbs beyond.

One of the suburbs north of Plano that has experienced tremendous growth in recent decades is Frisco, which has recently become something of an emerging sports center in the northern Metroplex with the construction of new state-of-the-art venues for the minor league Frisco Rough Riders baseball team and FC Dallas, the local professional soccer team. Located just across the street from the new baseball stadium is Stonebriar Centre Mall, one of the newest in the area. It has over 160 stores, including such national chains as Nordstrom, Macy's, and Barnes & Noble. The mall is located at the intersection of Preston Road and State Highway 121. It also includes a large ice rink and 24-screen movie theater. Twenty years ago, this new entertainment and shopping complex was little more than undeveloped farmland, but today it is surrounded by expanding residential communities.

Highland Park Village

Some fifty years after the city of Dallas was first officially chartered in 1906, John Armstrong purchased a large plot of land north of the city center with the intention of laying out a new community. He conceived his new community from the beginning as one that would adhere to uniformly high standards and a careful layout under the supervision of the city planner Wilbur David Cook, who also designed Beverly Hills. Much of the subsequent development of the new town of Highland Park was left to Armstrong's two sons-in-law, Hugh Prather and Edgar Flippen. Those plans did not receive wide endorsement from Dallas's financial leaders because they seemed to fly in the face of the accepted wisdom that the area's retail center would always be in Downtown Dallas. It should be noted that some of these doubters were probably also among those Dallas voters who rejected Highland Park's early bid to be annexed by Dallas.

Undaunted, Flippen and Prather decided to develop their center anyway and hired architects Marion Foosher and James Cheek to create a distinctive shopping enclave to serve as a Downtown Highland Park. The architects settled on a Spanish Colonial style and in 1931, Highland Park Village opened as the first self-contained shopping center in America. Unlike other shopping areas, particularly those located in business and financial districts of major cities, all of the shops in Highland Park Village were of the same architectural style and all faced away from the surrounding streets. Recently the entire center was placed on the National Register of Historic Places. It remains the social and commercial center of Highland Park, located at the corner of Preston Road and Mockingbird Lane, only a short few blocks from the Dallas Country Club. Its architecture has remained, with some renovation, true to its original design and the vision of its founders.

Beyond Big D:
Attractions in the Metroplex

International Terminal D at DFW Airport

The Dallas/Fort Worth area has never been shy about creating projects that are big in terms of conception and size. A case in point is the new International Terminal D at the Dallas/Fort Worth International Airport. The terminal is the newest and largest at the airport and is in fact the first major expansion undertaken by any airport in the country since 9/11. It measures over one million square feet and cost over $1 billion. The concession area, including gourmet restaurants and specialty boutiques, covers over 100,000 square feet. The security system is state-of-the-art and the ticketing counters can accommodate 32,000 passengers daily.

However, these amenities, welcome as they might be, do not really sum up everything the terminal has to offer the travelers who disembark from all parts of the globe. The greatest contribution the terminal has to offer may well be the many works of art that have been contributed by over 30 local, national, and international artists. Paintings, sculpture, and uniquely designed large medallions in the terminals's terrazzo floors bring an art museum feel to the airport. Included are such examples of Texas art as Terry Allen's massive bronze sculpture *Wishbone*, which measures 20 feet by 12 feet, and Fort Worth painter Dennis Blagg's 14-feet-by-42-feet landscape painting of Boquillas Canyon from the Big Bend region of far West Texas. From a distance the painting appears to be one large landscape; however, upon close inspection the painting turns out to be composed of 2,335 six-inch panels.

Previous page: Dallas Arboretum.

Texas Town. This 2.5-acre national award–winning exhibit features seven gardens that introduce the importance of plants for pioneer survival. The interactive exhibit includes an authentic sod house, two replica cabins, a covered wagon, and a Native American tepee.

Dallas Arboretum

Everett L. DeGolyer left many legacies including two world-class libraries, one at the University of Oklahoma and one at Southern Methodist University. He was a pioneer in the field of seismic oil exploration and at one time was the leading petroleum exploration consultant in the world. Born in a sod house on the Kansas prairie, DeGolyer and his wife, Nell, built a sprawling Spanish mansion on 44 acres overlooking White Rock Lake. DeGolyer died in 1956, leaving his collection of books and maps on Southwestern history to SMU. After the death of his wife in 1977, the entire estate was left to the university. The city of Dallas purchased the estate amid plans to create the Dallas Arboretum. A few years later, the adjoining Camp estate covering 22 acres was also acquired, and in 1982, the entire 66 acres, including both the DeGolyer and Camp houses, opened as the Dallas Arboretum.

Today the Arboretum boasts several specialty gardens, active educational programs that feature classes, demonstrations and workshops, and a popular weekly music series on Thursday evenings in the spring, summer, and fall. It is one of the city's most refreshing diversions. Each spring, thousands of visitors converge on the Arboretum for the annual Dallas Blooms festival that includes 400,000 tulips in bloom. The Arboretum now boasts a new educational center in addition to the DeGolyer and Camp houses. Sculptures and fountains have been placed throughout the gardens and thematic exhibitions can often be found scattered about the grounds. A man of diverse interests and talents, Everett DeGolyer had once considered the idea of establishing a botanical garden. Fittingly, that dream was later realized on his own estate.

Frontiers of Flight Museum

During World War II, Dallas's Love Field was home to the 601st Division of the Women's Army Service Pilots, or WASPS, who were charged with the task of ferrying the bombers and fighter planes from nearby factories in the Dallas/Fort Worth area to the fields of combat in Europe and Asia. The role of these brave women is just one of the topics covered at the Frontiers of Flight Museum, which opened in 2004, adjacent to the airport. The museum is housed in a 100,000-square-foot structure that resembles a giant aircraft hangar, much like the ones that used to house B-29 bombers on the same site.

The museum's 20 galleries cover the whole range of world aviation from the Wright Brothers to contemporary space flight. One of the galleries contains an exhaustive display on lighter-than-air aircraft, including several items from the ill-fated German zeppelin, the *Hindenburg*. Other galleries specifically deal with the contributions to aviation provided by the men, women, and corporations of the Metroplex.

At any given time, the museum displays over 25 full-size aircraft from a variety of historic periods, including the *Apollo 7* Command Module. The museum also offers an extensive program of educational experiences for children

Ryan PT-22 "Recruit": With the rapid expansion of the U.S. Air Force in 1941 came an increase in the need to train pilots and aircrews. In that year, Ryan Aeronautical received orders for the PT-22, officially named "Recruit." This was to be the major production model of the "Recruit," with 1,023 built. On loan from Carl and Darci Neuzil.

including classes, demonstrations, and an opportunity to attend a specially designed "flight school." The museum is active in the area of aviation research and history and has established a partnership with the University of Texas at Dallas to form and maintain the George E. Haddaway History of Aviation Collection. The collection contains a wide range of historic photographs, documents, and artifacts.

Apollo 7 Command Module: The first flight of the Apollo Program was accomplished by Walter Cunningham, Walter Schirra, and Donn Eisele in this spacecraft from October 11 to 22, 1968. Following the tragic fire that killed the three crewmen of Apollo 1, the Apollo spacecraft was extensively redesigned. All of the systems and procedures required for the moon mission were flight tested for the first time with this vehicle during its 163 Earth orbits in 10 days 20 hours 9 minutes, traveling a total distance of 4,539,959 miles. On loan from the National Air & Space Museum of The Smithsonian Institution, Washington, D.C.

White Rock Lake

Built in 1911 as a source of water for the rapidly growing city of Dallas, White Rock Lake now provides a recreation haven in the middle of the city. It has long since ceased functioning as a municipal water supply, but the lake and its surrounding park with its 9.3 miles of trails is perhaps the city's most popular spot for joggers, bicyclers, and skaters. Any given day will find the trail surrounding the lake filled with runners, speed walkers, and people just out for a leisurely stroll. There are a number of competitive races throughout the year for the more serious runners, including the White Rock Marathon in December.

The park and lake contain over 5,000 acres. Many of the recreational facilities were built in the 1930s through the Civilian Conservation Corps, a public works program established by President Franklin Roosevelt to put people back to work during the Great Depression. Many of those facilities have been updated in recent years, including the Bath House Cultural Center, which began as a bath house and now serves as a performance and visual arts center. The lake itself beckons many boating enthusiasts, but strict horsepower requirements limit most of the watercraft to sailboats or kayaks. Swimming is prohibited, but fishing (with some limitations) is allowed.

The lake is located about ten miles north of Downtown Dallas and surrounded by residential neighborhoods. Easily accessible from all parts of the city, White Rock is one of Dallas's best-known landmarks. In addition to picnicking and boating, park visitors can avail themselves of the wisdom of the "free advice guys." Neal Caldwell and Roger MacElwain can be found along the trail around the lake on most Sundays when the weather is good. They have been dispensing free advice on any topic to passersby for the last ten years. As their name implies, all advice is free, simply for the asking.

Lee Park

In 1903, a nickel would buy a streetcar ride from Downtown Dallas to a new park and recreation area developed by the owners of the Dallas Consolidated Electric Street Railway Company. The company partnered with real estate developers to attract new residents to the area. The idea worked so well that in six short years the city of Dallas bought the park and named it Oak Lawn Park. Numerous recreational facilities were later added, including a large pavilion, playgrounds, tennis courts, and a wading pool.

In the 1930s, the park went through another metamorphosis when the Dallas Southern Memorial Association raised $50,000 to commission nationally acclaimed sculptor A. Phimster Proctor to create a monumental tribute to Confederate General Robert E. Lee. In 1936,

President Franklin Roosevelt traveled to Dallas both to officially open the Texas Centennial Exposition in Fair Park and to dedicate the new statue. The park was officially renamed Lee Park to commemorate the event. The Memorial Association also raised another $30,000 to build Arlington Hall, a community center modeled after Lee's ancestral home and designed by prominent Dallas architect Mark Lemmon.

In an effort to bring the park and Arlington Hall back to their former glory, the Lee Park and Arlington Hall Conservancy was formed in 1995 for a $3 million campaign to restore Arlington Hall. It reopened in 2003, and the Conservancy now has plans to build several new gardens in the park.

Reverchon Park

Reverchon Park began in 1915 when the city of Dallas purchased 36 acres along Turtle Creek. At the time the park was called Turtle Creek Park and was located far from the city center. It was envisioned as Dallas's version of New York's Central Park. The park was renamed to honor early Dallas botanist Julie Reverchon, who had originally migrated from France with his father to join the utopian colony La Reunion near present-day Oak Cliff. When Reverchon and his father arrived in 1856, they discovered that the colony had already failed, but the two decided to stay in the area and purchased a farm. Throughout the rest of his life, Reverchon collected and catalogued thousands of species and specimens of Texas plant life.

The park named in his honor is part of a greenbelt along Turtle Creek that also includes Lee Park. Located near Maple and Oak Lawn, Reverchon boasts a number of city-operated athletic and recreational facilities. The developing KATY hiking and biking trail, built along the original right of way of the Missouri, Kansas, and Texas Railroad, has two entry points in Reverchon Park. In 2002, the nearby Scottish Rite Hospital for Children partnered with the city of Dallas to develop an innovative playground for children of all ability levels. The hospital was also instrumental in forming the Friends of Reverchon Park, which has spearheaded efforts to rehabilitate many of the park's features and structures that were built during the 1920s and 1930s, including the baseball field that was the first lighted facility in Dallas.

Six Flags Over Texas

When Dallas attorney and oilman Angus Wynne first conceived the idea for building a new amusement park midway between Dallas and Fort Worth, the city of Arlington was hardly an entertainment mecca. Wynne visited Disneyland in the late 1950s and thought that a similarly family-oriented park would prove popular in the Dallas area. Looking for a way to differentiate his idea from Walt Disney's vision, Wynne decided to develop the park around the concept of the six nations that had governed Texas—Spain, France, Mexico, the Republic of Texas, the Confederate States of America, and the United States. When Six Flags Over Texas opened in 1961, it was divided into six sections, each corresponding to one of those countries, with rides and other attractions tied to the specific cultures of each nation.

There is some evidence to suggest that Wynne was as interested in building up an adjacent business park as he was in developing an amusement park. By the end of the first year of operation, it was evident, however, that Six Flags would be wildly successful. Wynne earned his entire investment back in that first year. Both the park and Arlington have grown and changed substantially over the last 45 years. Arlington is now the largest city in the Metroplex outside of Dallas and Fort Worth and is the home of many entertainment venues, including Ameriquest Field, adjacent to Six Flags and the home of the major league baseball team the Texas Rangers. In 2009, the new Cowboys stadium will open nearby. Six Flags itself has grown from a single park to a corporation that manages several theme parks throughout the country. The original Six Flags Over Texas is still one of the most popular tourist attractions in the state. It is located just south of Interstate 30, almost equidistant from Dallas and Fort Worth.

Dallas World Aquarium and Zoological Garden

Located near the historic origin of Dallas, the Old Red Courthouse, and the red-brick warehouses of the West End, is a tropical rain forest and a penguin habitat. Close to the busy Woodall Rogers Freeway, the inhabitants of the Dallas World Aquarium and Zoological Garden are treated to a sophisticated climate-controlled environment that approximates the many regions of the world. The aquarium at 1801 Griffin Street in the heart of Downtown was first opened in 1993 and now contains 85,000 gallons of saltwater exhibits, including a 22,000 gallon tunnel that allows visitors a panoramic view life underneath a recreated reef.

The rain forest was added in 1997, with land and sea species including giant Australian clams (some weighing in excess of 300 pounds), crocodiles, boa constrictors, anacondas, and squirrel monkeys.

The facility was expanded for a third time in 2003 with the addition of the Mundo Maya exhibit that immerses visitors in the geography

The spectacled angelfish (Chaetodontoplus conspicillatus) *can be recognized by its striking coloration. The common name is derived from its blue "spectacles." The spectacled angelfish is one of the most highly prized species in the aquarium trade.*

and cultures covered by the ancient Mayan civilization and its modern descendants. The exhibit stretches over three levels, simulating the natural environment from the Yucatan peninsula to the interior of Mexico and the countries of Belize, Honduras, Guatemala, and El Salvador.

The aquarium is accredited by the American Association of Zoos and Aquaria and participates in numerous worldwide conservation efforts. Among its displays is a breeding pair of Orinoco crocodiles from Venezuela. In turn, the aquarium supports many conservation efforts in Venezuela along with several other zoos.

Dallas Zoo

Dallas's first zoo began modestly, but early, with only four animals, two deer, and two mountain lions. The zoo was founded in 1888, making it the oldest zoo in Texas. It was originally located in a city park (now the site of Dallas Heritage Village) and moved to its present location in Oak Cliff in 1912. Today, the zoo is the largest in Texas in terms of acreage, and one of the most active in terms of research and educational programs. It is divided into two major areas, Zoo North and the Wilds of Africa. The latter is part of a multimillion-dollar expansion project that created a 25-acre tract covering the six primary African habitats: bush, river, forest, desert, mountain, and woodland. The African exhibit has been rated as one of the best in America and includes more than 80 species that live in settings that closely approximate

American flamingoes are exhibited at the Dallas Zoo.

Left: Lowland Gorilla.

Below: Okapi mother and baby.

African environments. A narrated monorail tour of the exhibit is available, but due to the Texas environment which includes searing summer temperatures often topping 100 degrees, it runs only in the more temperate days of spring and fall.

Among the highlights of Zoo North is the Exxon/Mobil Endangered Tiger Habitat that is designed to emulate a tropical rain forest that has recently undergone a logging operation.

Visitors to Zoo North can take time off from viewing some of the planet's largest mammals by visiting some of its smallest creatures in a new exhibit called "Bug U," which explores the world of Texas invertebrates. Zoo North also includes the Lacerte Family Children's Zoo which offers a number of interactive activities including a petting area.

The Dallas Zoo is located just east of I-35 about three miles from the city's center. Travelers along the freeway can easily detect the zoo's entrance by the 67-foot sculpture of a giraffe by artist Bob Cassilly.

Southfork Ranch

For millions of people around the world, the city of Dallas will always be represented by the television series of the same name that during its 13-year run played in 96 countries and was translated into 43 languages. The world of the television series had very little to do with the

real world of Dallas, but that did not stop the show from being the second-longest-running series in television history. Most of the series was filmed on a sound stage in Los Angeles. The real Dallas was used primarily as a backdrop, with a few exterior scenes filmed around the city to give some local authenticity. The fictional Ewing clan lived on a ranch just outside of the city. The ranch and its signature house were indeed located around twenty miles from the real Dallas, but the spread was in reality a mere 41 acres, not the purported 100,000 acres mentioned in the series.

So popular was the television series that the actual ranch used for exterior shots became one of the state's most popular tourist attractions. When more and more international airlines began operating out of DFW airport in the mid-1980s, a burgeoning tour business developed taking visitors from Europe, Asia, and parts in between to see where the Ewings lived. Although the series has been out of production for many years, Southfork still attracts a fair number of visitors each year to see the house made famous by J.R. and his family.

The sort of excess epitomized in the television show has been something of a blessing and a curse for the real Dallas. The stereotypes immortalized in the show were caricatures indeed, but their types were rooted in the "larger-than-life" image that had long been associated with Dallas, an image that many Dallasites carefully have fostered.

The living room in the Ewing Mansion at Southfork Ranch.

The Mustangs at Las Colinas Sculpture

Created over a seven-year period from 1977 to 1984, *The Mustangs at Las Colinas*, by sculptor Robert Glen, reminds visitors of the Western heritage of North Texas amid a 12,000-acre planned community of office buildings, golf courses, and residences. Las Colinas was once home to a 6,000-acre working cattle ranch located on the outskirts of Irving, just northwest of Dallas. Ben H. Carpenter decided to convert his family ranch into a gleaming community of skyscrapers, monorails, and canals shortly after the announcement of plans to locate the DFW Regional Airport just a short distance away. Las Colinas has undergone many ups and downs financially since the late 1970s when the sculpture was commissioned, but today the area is home to several Fortune 500 companies, including the world headquarters of Exxon/Mobil.

The nine wild mustangs depicted in the sculpture are one and one-half life-size and are displayed as if the herd is running across a stream. Specially designed nozzles were placed under the horses' hooves to give the illusion that the horses were in full gallop across the stream, which runs across a pink granite courtyard. Ironically, the sculpture which is designed to evoke a very southwestern slice of history was conceived and executed by an artist who was born in Kenya, lives in Nairobi, and is primarily known for depicting African wildlife. Glen spent a year in Spain studying the anatomy of Andalusian stallions because those horses were said to be the ancestors of the wild mustangs of the American Southwest. Glen modeled the sculptures in his Nairobi studio but had them cast in bronze at a foundry in London and finally shipped to Texas for installation.

Detail of The Mustangs at Las Colinas *sculpture.*

McKinney Town Square

Settlers began arriving in what is now McKinney at around the same time that John Neely Bryan was staking out his claim along the banks of the Trinity in 1841. Bryan's settlement became Dallas, and for well over a century McKinney was merely a pleasant farming community thirty miles to the north. The city was named the county seat after creation of Collin County in 1848. Both the town and county were named after a prominent early settler, Collin McKinney, who was a signer of the Texas Declaration of Independence. While Dallas became a center for transportation and business by the end of the nineteenth century, McKinney did not experience a significant growth spurt until the twenty-first century. The 2000 census listed the population of McKinney as a little over 50,000 people; by 2006 the population had topped 100,000, earning McKinney the distinction of being one of the fastest-growing cities in the nation.

While McKinney's growth has been spectacular in recent years, its citizens have taken care to preserve the community's historic character. The downtown square has an active Main Street program that has worked to preserve many of the buildings that were constructed over 100 years ago. The former Collin County Courthouse that dominates the town square has been extensively renovated and is now the McKinney Performing Arts Center. The town square also boasts several antique stores, boutiques, and restaurants. Some of the buildings on the square have also been converted into loft apartments. As more and more new residents relocate to this northern edge of the Dallas/Fort Worth Metroplex, the historic preservation efforts on display in the McKinney town square will serve as a testament to how a community can successfully retain a small-town atmosphere even with explosive population growth.

Denton Town Square

Located thirty miles north of Fort Worth and Dallas, Denton has primarily been known as the home to two institutions of higher learning: the University of North Texas and Texas Woman's University. Like several other communities at the northern reaches of the Metroplex, Denton, which was founded in 1857, has undergone dramatic and rapid growth in the last few years. The town is the county seat of Denton County, named for John Denton, an early settler and soldier, who is buried near the 1896 courthouse at the town center.

Today the courthouse contains a history museum that offers a glimpse of the area's past. Surrounding the courthouse is an eclectic array of antique stores, restaurants, and businesses that cater both to visitors drawn by the historic nature of the buildings and to the thousands of students from the nearby universities. One of the most popular businesses for both is Recycled Books, Records, and CDs, which boasts an inven-tory of over 200,000 books. Also of note on the square is Evers Hardware Store, which has been in operation since 1885. Like its neighbor to the east, McKinney, Denton has an active Main Street program that works to preserve the historical structures of the square. Over $20 million has been invested in historic preservation since the program's inception in 1989.

The Wright Opera House was built in 1901 with Denton-fired brick taken from the old county courthouse. The upper floor contained the opera house and public hall that seated 1,000 people. Denton's elite visited the Opera House for a few years until movies came to town.

Way Out West:
Cowboys and Culture
in Fort Worth

Tarrant County Courthouse

Fort Worth got its start as a frontier outpost in 1849. It was named after General William Jenkins Worth, a hero of the recent war between the United States and Mexico. It was a military encampment established to ward off attacks on settlers by the Comanche and Kiowa who had roamed over the area for many years and who still viewed the territory as rightfully theirs. First known as Camp Worth, its name was officially changed to Fort Worth only a few months after its establishment.

In less than a decade after its founding, the frontier line had already moved considerably farther to the west and Fort Worth was abandoned as a military fort, but the town was already attracting permanent settlers who decided to stay on even after the soldiers left. By the mid-1850s, Fort Worth served as a busy station on the stagecoach line taking travelers to California. Its Western and cowboy heritage was firmly established after the Civil War when an abundance of longhorn cattle in South Texas led to the great cattle drives.

Sitting on a bluff overlooking the Trinity River, the Tarrant County Courthouse is one of the most impressive nineteenth-century buildings remaining in modern Fort Worth. The courthouse was finished in 1895 for $408,000, an extraordinary cost at the time. Three decades earlier, the citizens of Fort Worth had vigorously fought for the distinction of being the county seat, an honor awarded the city in 1860. Two other courthouses, not nearly as ambitious as this one, were built earlier, but the latter of those was destroyed by fire, not an uncommon occurrence in those days. The present facility is built of Texas pink granite and bears a striking resemblance to the sate capitol in Austin, also constructed of the same stone. When it was completed, area citizens were outraged at its cost, so much so that they promptly voted every county commissioner out of office. Whether viewed as a costly extravagance or an appropriate edifice to local government, the building has remained a local landmark. It still functions today as a home to the county government.

It also anchors the north end of Downtown Fort Worth; to the north lies the Fort Worth Stockyards National Historic District, where the Western heritage side of the city is celebrated.

Previous page: Fort Worth Herd, the world's only daily cattle drive.

Fort Worth Water Gardens

Designed by architect Philip Johnson as an urban oasis, the Water Gardens located in the South End of Downtown Fort Worth near the Convention Center are indeed a spectacular addition to the city. When they opened in 1974, many locals thought the area was hardly an oasis. The problem was not the three signature water features spread over a nearly five-acre site. The problem was the lack of shade combined with the hot Texas sun and the great expanses of concrete, resulting in an urban park that most locals avoided in the summer. But over the ensuing years, Johnson's and his partner John Burgee's original vision has come to fruition as their landscape plan, which features an abundance of trees, has matured. The Water Gardens is today truly one garden with spectacular water features and much-needed shade.

The Water Gardens are a prime example of the sort of public/private partnership that has made Fort Worth a model for other cities. The city wanted to upgrade a portion of Downtown to complement the Convention Center. The Amon Carter Foundation helped the city acquire the land and then commissioned Johnson and Burgee to create the Water Gardens. The city now maintains the area, which is open free of charge.

Sundance Square

In the late 1860s and early 1870s, Texas cowboys began moving longhorn cattle from South Texas to the rail heads of Kansas. One of the main routes was the Chisholm Trail, which passed only a short distance from modern Downtown Fort Worth. The work was hard and dangerous and the trail was long, so naturally the cowboys were eager to afford themselves of whatever diversions the few towns along the route offered. In its early years, Fort Worth provided more than a few diversions; so many saloons grew up around the northern part of town and so many cowboys, gamblers, and others hung out in them that the area became known as "Hell's Half Acre." Reportedly among the notorious men who frequented the area were outlaws Butch Cassidy and the Sundance Kid.

Today the only remnants of those days are twenty blocks of largely restored turn-of-the-century buildings and Sundance's name. Overlooked by the Tarrant County Courthouse to the north, Sundance Square is now an entertainment, business, and residential district that features a splendid restoration of historic structures. An area that was once known to be one of the rowdiest places in the Southwest is now one of the finest examples of historic restoration and adaptive reuse, thanks to the generosity of the Bass Family, whose philanthropic pursuits can be seen all over the city, but nowhere more prominently than in Sundance Square. The area contains many restaurants, movie theaters, and the Sid W. Richardson Collection of Western Art. Visitors can also learn about the early days of both Forth Worth and Sundance Square by visiting Fire Station No. 1, which presents a history of the area. The museum is a branch of the Fort Worth Museum of Science and History, which is located in the nearby Cultural District.

Nancy Lee and Perry R. Bass Performance Hall

While Sundance Square is one of the country's best examples of historic restoration and renovation, not every venue in the area is a turn-of-the-century classic building. There are some new classics. The Nancy Lee and Perry R. Bass Performance Hall is a gift to the city of Fort Worth by philanthropists Nancy Lee and Perry Bass, and just one of the many attractions and amenities that the Bass family has provided for the city. Architect David Schwarz, who has designed many buildings and venues in the Dallas/Forth Worth area, has produced a building that, while new, fits nicely with the historic structures that surround it in Sundance Square.

The Hall opened in 1998, built completely with private funds. It has played host to classical, as well as popular musicians and is frequently the site of touring Broadway productions. Its resident companies include the Forth Worth Symphony, Fort Worth Opera, and the Texas Ballet Theater. Every four years, the Hall is the site of the Van Cliburn International Piano Competition.

Many of the building's interior and exterior materials are from Texas; some are even from the Fort Worth area. Its most prominent exterior adornments are two 48-foot-tall angels carved from Texas limestone. The Hall has a little over 2,000 seats.

Amon Carter Museum

Three remarkable men have combined their talents to create the Amon Carter Museum: the founding collector, Amon Carter; the architect, Philip Johnson; and the museum's founding director, Mitchell Wilder. Carter was one of Fort Worth's and Texas's most legendary men. The publisher of the *Fort Worth Star-Telegram* and a successful oilman, Carter began collecting the art of the American West, primarily the work of the genre's greatest artists, Frederic Remington and Charles M. Russell, in 1935. Ten years later, he acquired Remington's early masterpiece, *A Dash for the Timber.*

After his death, his estate funded the creation of a museum to house his collection in 1955. His wishes were carried out by his son, Amon Carter, Jr., and daughter, Ruth Carter Stevenson, who still serves as the president of the museum's board.

Philip Johnson was chosen as the architect. The building opened in 1961 and Johnson's third expansion was opened in 2001, culminating a remarkable 40-year cycle of design and construction. The building has grown from its original concept as a "jewel box" constructed of Texas shell stone to its present 109,000 square feet. The most recent addition was built on the site of Johnson's second addition of 1977. The building expansion represents the steady growth of the museum's permanent collections and its world-class research library devoted to Western history and art.

The Amon Carter Museum now holds one of the country's premier collections of American art, encompassing a wide range of nineteenth- and twentieth-century paintings, drawings, prints, and sculpture, as well as photographs from the earliest days of the medium to the present.

The museum's first director, Mitchell Wilder, quickly set a groundbreaking course for the museum by asserting that the museum would be devoted to "the Westering of America." Wilder believed that the study of the impact of the West on American culture, history, and art was essential to understanding the American character. He also believed that Western American art should be viewed in the context of American art and culture in general. Consequently, the museum expanded its collecting parameters beyond the most traditional examples of Western art, began an ambitious publishing and exhibition program, and established one of the country's finest collections of American photography. Wilder formed a synthesis with Carter's original collecting vision, Johnson's aesthetic, and his

own understanding of American history and culture to create a programming vision that has frequently pushed the envelope of how the American West is viewed and interpreted.

Kimbell Art Museum

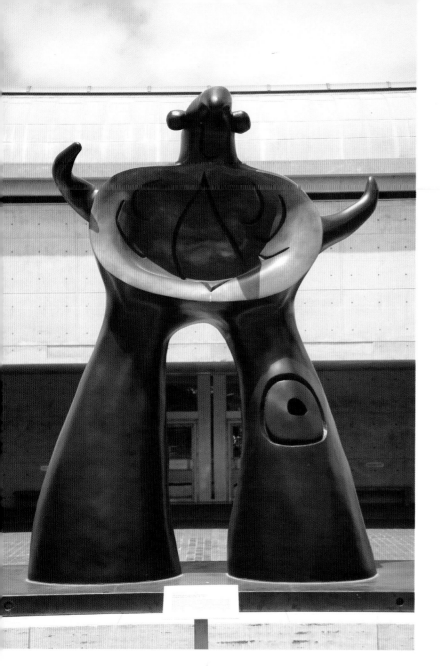

Few museum buildings have opened to such universal praise from the public and the architectural community as Fort Worth's Kimbell Art Museum, which opened across the street from the Amon Carter Museum in 1972. It was Louis Kahn's last design and most critics have deemed it his best. In fact, fans have said and continue to say that it is the best-designed museum building in the world. Its sixteen vaults appear to be laid on their sides, allowing the museum to be diffused almost entirely in natural light. When museum staff and board members have hinted on more than one occasion that they were considering a museum expansion, the architectural world has erupted in protest. The universal feeling seems to be that the building is a truly unique treasure that should not be altered in any way.

Woman Addressing the Public
by Joan Miró 1980–1981.

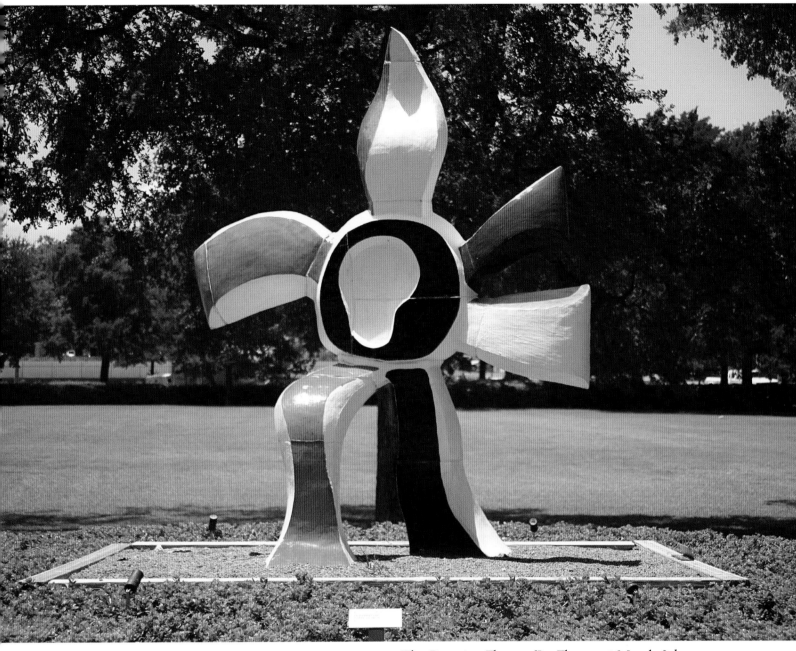

The Running Flower (La Fleur qui Marche) *by Fernand Léger, 1952, The Burnett Foundation, Fort Worth.*

The museum was created through the will and estate of Fort Worth businessman Kay Kimbell and his wife Velma. The couple had collected art from around the world for several years. When Kimbell died in 1964, he left instructions in his will to create a first-class museum. His widow then dedicated his entire estate to that purpose, thus creating one of the nation's largest endowments for an art museum.

Richard Fargo Brown was hired as the director in 1965 and guided the board to create a vision for the early museum. Brown worked closely with Kahn in developing the museum's building.

Although the Kimbells left their collection to the museum, they left no requirements about which pieces should be displayed or even retained. Consequently, the museum has had great resources from the very beginning to acquire works of art of the highest quality. Under the direction of Brown and his successor, Ted Pillsbury, the museum has built an impressive collection that spans a wide range of historic periods and genres.

Deborah Butterfield, Hina, 1990–91, unique bronze, 80 x 112 x 28 inches, Collection of the Modern Art Museum of Fort Worth, museum purchase, made possible by a gift from Web Maddox Trust acquired 1992.

Modern Art Museum of Fort Worth

Three years before the present Tarrant County Courthouse was built and a decade before the Livestock Exchange Building opened in the Fort Worth Stockyards National Historic District, Texas's first art museum was established. In 1892, the Fort Worth Public Library and Art Gallery was chartered. It has undergone several name changes over the last century and is now known as the Modern Art Museum of Fort Worth. Its collection is focused on art in the post–World War II era. Ironically the state's first art museum and the first museum to be located in Fort Worth's Cultural District is home to one of the state's most contemporary collections and certainly one of its most modern buildings.

When the trustees of the museum decided that the museum needed more space to accommodate its growing collection and a new building that would have a similar stature with two neighboring museums, the Amon Carter and the Kimbell, they faced a daunting task. Six international architects were invited to submit design proposals.

The unanimous choice was Japanese architect Tadao Ando. His building, which opened in 2002, is proof that the museum's trustees made a wise choice. It has been acclaimed as one of the most stunning museum designs in recent years and it sits easily next to Louis Kahn's Kimbell Art Museum and Philip Johnson's Amon Carter Museum.

All three museums are regarded as among the finest in the nation. Each has built a unique reputation and each pursues a unique program that does not encroach upon the collecting interests or programs of the other. The Carter's focus is on American art and photography. Its art collection is confined to pre-1945 work. The Modern looks to work in the postwar era, and the Kimbell directs its attention to many different periods of world art and antiquities.

View looking north of the Modern Art Museum of Fort Worth's new building, designed by Japanese architect Tadao Ando, opened to the public on Saturday, December 14, 2002.

Fort Worth Museum of Science and History

The Fort Worth Museum of Science and History can boast of a number of firsts: it was the first children's museum in Texas, the first museum in the state to operate a preschool, and the first museum in Texas to build a domed IMAX theater in 1983, the OmniMax. The museum was founded in 1945, and its main focus has always been on education, with a strong emphasis on teaching children.

The museum was instructing schoolchildren about Texas history and natural history, astronomy, and science in general long before its home on Fort Worth's West Side was dubbed a Cultural District. It features over 60 interactive exhibits and partners with such nationally known institutions as San Francisco's Exploratorium in developing innovative learning experiences for people of all ages.

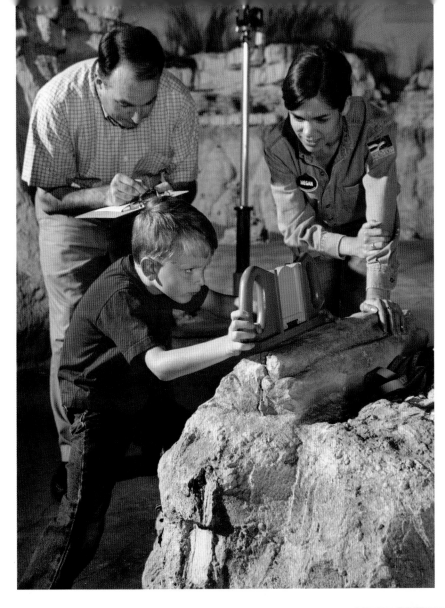

The Fort Worth Museum of Science and History's Lone Star Dinosaurs exhibit allows guests to use the real tools and skills of paleontology to make their own discoveries. It features five new species of dinosaur found in North Texas.

In years past, the museum has been overshadowed somewhat by world-class art museums that also call the Cultural District home. However, it has recently embarked on a $65 million capital campaign to build a new museum designed by Mexico City architect Ricardo Legorreta, known for his use of bright colors and unusual angles. The new museum will be built on the same site as the old one and will incorporate the OmniMax Theater. During the construction phase, the museum will utilize temporary buildings provided by the Fort Worth Independent School District as administrative and classroom space. The nearby National Cowgirl Museum and Hall of Fame will host its temporary exhibits.

The museum's outdoor DinoDig area is popular with young visitors, who can dig for real fossils then take them home!

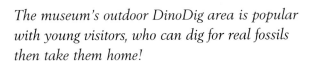

National Cowgirl Museum and Hall of Fame

Fort Worth has long celebrated its cowboy heritage, but only since 2002 has it had an institution that is devoted to the women of the American West. The National Cowgirl Museum and Hall of Fame is dedicated to all of the women who have made singular contributions to the history and culture of the West. The museum was founded in Hereford, a small ranching community in the Texas Panhandle in 1975, but its founders began looking for a larger community to showcase its expanding collections in the early 1990s. Fort Worth was chosen as the new location both because of its celebrated Western history and the financial support pledged by several civic leaders. Architect David Schwarz was chosen to design the building, adding to the long list of cultural and sporting

venues he has contributed to the Dallas/Fort Worth area.

The museum is located in the city's Cultural District and is close to the Will Rogers Coliseum, which was built as part of the 1936 Texas Frontier Centennial Exposition. Schwarz was challenged to create a new structure that would complement the nearby coliseum and one that could also be expanded to accommodate the future growth of the museum. The museum inducts new honorees into the Hall of Fame each year and also produces temporary exhibitions on several Western topics. Permanent exhibitions focus on many aspects of Western history and culture, from ranching to entertainment. The institution also maintains a research library and archives on women's history.

A 45-foot-high domed rotunda serves as a constant orienting point and houses the Hall of Fame Honoree exhibits.

Casa Mañana Theater

Never willing to be outdone by anything happening in Dallas, Forth Worth publisher and promoter Amon Carter was appalled when Dallas won the honor of hosting the Texas Centennial Exposition Exposition in 1936. Carter made a habit of carrying his lunch when he visited Dallas to avoid actually buying a meal there. His response to the centennial celebration held in Dallas was to stage a simultaneous event in Fort Worth which bore the title of the Texas Frontier Centennial Exposition. While the Fort Worth event included a number of historical and agriculture-related exhibits, its centerpiece and main attractions were decidedly in the entertainment area. Famous burlesque star Sally Rand was one of the headliners, but even more spectacular than Rand's fan dances was Casa Mañana, an outdoor theater in the round that sat 3,500 people around a revolving stage that appeared to float over a pool of water.

The theater operated for only two years, 1936 and 1937, but twenty years later, in 1958, a new theater on a somewhat less grand scale was built on the same spot. Like its predecessor, this theater was designed specifically for theater-in-the-round performances. Its design was based on Buckminster Fuller's concept of a geodesic dome. In 2003, the theater was renovated and the theater-in-the-round concept was modified to include a more traditional stage; but the dome still remains.

Trinity Trails

While Fort Worth is rich in history and cultural attractions, it is also fortunate to have an abundance of parks and greenbelts, many of which are linked with over 35 miles of hiking and biking paths known as Trinity Trails. The system stretches from the far southwest of the city to its northeastern edge, connecting the historic Stockyards area to Downtown and to parks accessible to both the Botanic Garden and the Fort Worth Zoo.

In the not-too-distant future, the system will be enlarged with the addition of 60 miles of new trails, part of Fort Worth's grand plan for the development of the Trinity River Watershed.

These plans, which were adopted in 2003, call for a new bypass channel to be built, replacing the aging levee system as a means of flood control. The channel will be located in the northeast area of the city near the Stockyards, allowing for new parks and residential and retail developments. The present trail system will link up with the new development, allowing joggers and bikers to tour the entire city without automobiles. Both Fort Worth and Dallas are involved in massive urban revitalization projects to utilize the Trinity River as a major source of economic development and enhanced recreational opportunities.

Above: Golden Moon Bridge in the Japanese Garden.
Opposite: Lily pond in the Fuller Garden.

Fort Worth Botanic Garden

Now spread over 109 acres, the Fort Worth Botanic Garden began in the middle of the Great Depression as a public works project. Initially, the garden was composed entirely of a formal rose garden that reflected a formalized European arrangement and layout. Since then the garden, which is the oldest botanic garden in the state, has diversified to include 21 different gardens.

There are now two rose gardens, the lower rose garden and the oval rose garden. In 1970, a seven-acre Japanese Garden was added and has become one of the area's most popular features.

Many of the Botanic Garden's more exotic species are found in a 10,000-square-foot conser-

vatory. In all, the Garden has 2,500 native Texas and exotic plants. The Water Conservation Garden instructs visitors on which plants are best adapted to the Texas climate, particularly those that flourish in a semi-arid climate. The Trial Garden offers a glimpse into how plants are selected for the various gardens. If plants do well in this setting, they are transferred to the other thematic areas. Other senses in addition to sight are also taken into consideration when planning the gardens. For example, the Fragrance Garden is designed for visitors to enjoy a wide variety of fragrances, some of which are only released when a plant's leaves are rubbed.

Fort Worth Zoo

Dallas can boast of having the first zoo in Texas, but Fort Worth can say that it has the distinction of having operated a zoo in the same location for the longest period of time of any zoo in the state. The Fort Worth Zoo was founded as a city-run facility in 1909 with only a few animals, including a lion and two bear cubs. The city operated the zoo for 82 years until the private Fort Worth Zoological Association assumed management through a contract with the city. Since then, over $70 million of private funds have been raised to improve exhibits and other amenities. Today the zoo is ranked among the best in the nation (along with its counterpart in Dallas) and attracts around a million visitors each year.

American flamingoes (pictured here), Chilean flamingoes, and other species of flamingo are exhibited at the Fort Worth Zoo.

The Zoo now boasts over 435 different species, including one of the largest collections of reptiles in the United States. In addition to the herpetarium, the zoo has exhibits on primates, including rare bonobos (pygmy chimpanzees), an African savannah, and a Komodo dragon habitat. One of its newest areas is Texas Wild, which focuses on the geography, natural habitats, and wildlife of the Lone Star State. The Zoo is open 365 days a year.

An endangered species, the Indochinese tiger is part of a national breeding program to establish a self-sustaining and genetically healthy population of tigers in North American zoos.

The green mamba is one of 135 species in the Fort Worth Zoo's world-famous reptile collection.

Cowtown Coliseum

When it was built in 1908, cowboys were no longer trailing herds of longhorns up the Chisholm Trail, but there were still plenty of cowboys to be found in and around the Cowtown Coliseum in Forth Worth's Stockyards National Historic District. Buying and selling cattle along with processing the beef at two nearby packing plants were primary activities around the Coliseum. Although it was the site of the first indoor rodeo in 1918 and has seen numerous rodeo performances since then, the Coliseum was built as a general-purpose exhibition and event venue, not just a site for Western-themed performances. The Coliseum at one time was the chief cultural venue for the city of Fort Worth. Presidents from Theodore Roosevelt to Jimmy Carter have addressed audiences there and performers have ranged from Enrico Caruso to Elvis Presley.

Today, the Coliseum is an entertainment mainstay of the Stockyards District and most of its activities are Western-related, including a modern version of Pawnee Bill's Wild West Show. Every weekend features the Stockyards Championship Rodeo where present-day cowboys compete in traditional events including bull riding, which was introduced at the Coliseum back in 1934. On any given day, the Coliseum is likely to be hosting some sort of entertainment event, most of which directly relate to the Western heritage and historic nature of the area. As for the longhorns, a small herd parades past the Coliseum every day.

Opposite page: Stockyards Championship Rodeo at Cowtown Coliseum, home of the first indoor rodeo.

Grapevine Vintage Railroad

Like that of Dallas, Fort Worth's early history was greatly affected by the arrival of the railroads. Fort Worth became a center for the cattle industry because the railroads provided the means to get Texas cattle to markets in the north and east. Later, after meatpackers Swift and Armour were persuaded to build plants adjacent to the Livestock Exchange Building where cattle were auctioned off daily, refrigerated boxcars carried Texas steaks and other prime cuts to restaurants and markets all across the country.

In the late nineteenth and early twentieth centuries, many different rail lines headed off in almost every direction from the central core of Fort Worth. So many were built that some locals began referring to the network as a tarantula, since a map of the lines resembled the legs of a spider. Most of those lines have long since ceased serving passengers, but one does remain. The Grapevine Vintage Railroad operates daily excursions on vintage equipment between the northern Metroplex city of Grapevine and Fort Worth's Stockyards National Historic District. It also runs another excursion from the Stockyards along the Trinity River to Downtown Fort Worth and back. The train follows the Cotton Belt Route which was originally established in 1877. The trip from Grapevine to the Stockyards is a mere 21 miles in distance, but it covers more than a century of history.

Billy Bob's Texas

Some country-and-western clubs have mechanical bulls: Billy Bob's Texas, which bills itself as the world's largest honky tonk, has real bulls. Having a professional bull riding arena within the cavernous confines of the club is only appropriate because the building was first built in 1910 as an open-air showplace for the prize cattle from the annual Fort Worth Stock Show. In 1936, the building was modernized with the inclusion of a roof; its main function though was still a showcase for livestock. Over the next few decades, the building had some very diverse uses, from serving as an aircraft factory in World War II to housing a department store in the 1950s. Its present incarnation began in 1981, and since that time over fifteen million visitors have taken their turns on the dance floor, listened to such top country acts as Willie Nelson, cheered on the bull riders, or simply marveled at the sheer size of this 127,000-square-foot entertainment complex.

Billy Bob's is north of the Cowtown Coliseum in the Fort Worth Stockyards National Historic District, so naturally much of its entertainment offerings have a Western flavor. However, it is also host to other musical genres and performances. It is frequently used as a setting for television and movie productions, as well as music videos.

Livestock Exchange Building and the Fort Worth Stockyards

In 1903, Fort Worth was rapidly developing into one of the leading livestock markets in the nation, not only for cattle, but also for pork, sheep, mules, and horses. It consistently ranked behind only Chicago and Kansas City in terms of beef sales (by World War II, it would surpass both cities in that category). Swift and Armour had major meatpacking facilities in the city's North Side and several smaller companies were also operating livestock businesses near the Stockyards. So much business was being conducted in the area that the Fort Worth Stockyards National Historic District built a two-story Spanish-style building on Exchange Avenue to house all of the various related operations. The Livestock Exchange Building quickly became the heart of the entire Stockyards area. It was the very center of what some people called the "Wall Street of the West."

Over a century since its construction, the building is still the heart of the Fort Worth Stockyards National Historic District. The building is home to the Stockyards Museum, operated by the North Fort Worth Historical Society, that gives an overview of the area's colorful history. It also serves a commercial purpose as an office space for a wide variety of businesses, some still related to livestock trading. Cattle auctions are no longer a staple of the adjacent cattle pens that have been standing since the late nineteenth century. Tourists from all over the world now wander over the brick floors of the cattle and horse pens and barns, bringing another kind of commerce to the area. In its original heyday, the Stockyards District was one of the busiest livestock markets in the country; today it is one of the busiest tourist attractions in Texas.

A magnificent bronze statue portraying Bill Pickett throwing a Longhorn, by Lisa Perry. Pickett was the first African-American cowboy to be inducted into the Cowboy Hall of Fame. He appeared at the Cowtown Coliseum when it opened in 1908.

Sid W. Richardson Collection of Western Art

Fort Worth oilman Sid W. Richardson and newspaper publisher Amon Carter were great friends who shared many interests, including collecting art of the American West, particularly works by the two best-known artists of the Old West, Frederic Remington and Charles M. Russell. Sometimes their friendship turned into a friendly rivalry when it came to competing for the same paintings. Carter amassed the larger collection, but Richardson's contains some of the finest examples of the work of both Remington and Russell. The Amon Carter Museum opened in 1961, in what is now known as the Cultural District. For a while, both Carter's and Richardson's collections were displayed there.

When Richardson's nephew, Perry R. Bass, and his family began redeveloping Downtown Fort Worth, plans were made to adapt a building specifically to display the Richardson art collection. The Sid W. Richardson Collection of Western Art was one of the first buildings to be renovated in Sundance Square and has since undergone an expansion project to provide more space for educational activities. Much of the small museum's permanent Western collection is on display throughout the year.

Appropriately, the paintings and sculpture depicting the history of the cattle trade are on view only a short distance from where cowboys drove their steers toward the open range of Montana more than a century ago, the range where Russell himself once worked as a night wrangler.

$\mathcal{I}ndex$

A
Airports
  Dallas/Fort Worth International Airport, 6, 110
  International Terminal D at Dallas/Fort
    Worth International Airport, 6, 22–23, 110
  Love Field, 8, 112

B
Bass, Perry R., 158
Boll, Henri (Doctor), 34
Bryan, John Neely, 8–10, 26, 28, 125
Buildings
  Bank of America Plaza, 60, 62
  Bank One Center, 63
  Crescent Court, 67
  Dallas City Hall, 71, 82
  Hall of State, 11, 42, 52
  J. P. Morgan/Chase Tower, 60
  Livestock Exchange Building, 140, 154, 156
  Magnolia Building, 56–57, 68
  Old Red Courthouse, 26, 28, 118
  Renaissance Tower, 61
  Reunion Tower, 68
  Tarrant County Courthouse, 22, 130, 133, 140
  Union Station, 39
  Wilson Building, 72

C
Carter, Amon, 14, 16, 136–137, 146, 158
Cemeteries
  Freedman's Cemetery Memorial, 32–33
Churches
  Cathedral Santuario de Guadalupe, 22, 60, 84
Cities
  Arlington, 21, 22, 53, 97, 98, 100, 117
  Denton, 21, 87, 90, 126–127
  Fort Worth, 90, 130
  Frisco, 21, 106
  Irving, 19, 21, 88, 97, 124
  McKinney, 125
  University Park, 67, 93, 103, 106
Colleges and universities
  Southern Methodist University, 52, 91–93, 103, 111
  Texas Christian University, 89
  Texas Woman's University, 87, 126
  University of Dallas, 88
  University of North Texas, 90, 126
  University of Texas at Dallas, 113
Cotton Belt Route, 154

D
Dallas
  African-American settlement, 32
  Origin of name, 10
Dallas Area Rapid Transit (DART), 7, 19, 21, 39, 99
Dallas Arts District, 22, 51, 60, 67, 70, 76, 77, 78, 82, 83, 85
Dallas County Heritage Society, 31
Dallas Morning News, 29
Dallas Symphony Orchestra, 82
Dallas Trade Center, 80
Dallas, Alexander (Commodore), 10

Dallas, George Mifflin (Vice President), 10
Denton, John, 126

F
Fort Worth Opera, 134
Forth Worth Symphony, 134

G
Grapevine Vintage Railroad, 154

H
Historic homes
  Southfork Ranch, 122–123
Hotels
  Adolphus Hotel, 58–59

J
Johnson, Philip, 19, 22, 28, 60, 63, 64, 67, 131, 136, 137

K
Kahn, Louis, 19, 138, 139, 140
Kennedy, John F. (President), 17, 20, 28, 71

L
La Reunion, 34, 69
Legorreta, Ricardo, 86, 143
Libraries
  Dallas Public Library, 39
  George W. Bush Presidential Library, 88

M
Markets
  Dallas Farmer's Market, 57, 66
  Highland Park Village, 107
  NorthPark Center, 20, 79, 102
  Snider Plaza, 103
  Stonebriar Centre Mall, 106
Metroplex
  Population statistics, 22
Monuments and memorials
  Freedman's Cemetery Memorial, 32–33
  Hall of Heroes, 42
  John F. Kennedy Memorial, 28–29, 63
  Thanksgiving Memorial, 64–65
Museums
  African American Museum, 32, 45
  Age of Steam Railroad Museum, 46
  Amon Carter Museum, 19, 63, 87, 136, 140, 158
  Dallas Heritage Village, 30–31, 120
  Dallas Historical Society, 42
  Dallas Museum of Art, 19, 76
  Fort Worth Museum of Science and
    History, 133, 142–143
  Frontiers of Flight Museum, 112
  Kimbell Art Museum, 19, 22, 138–139, 140
  Latino Cultural Center, 86
  Meadows Museum, 91–93
  Modern Art Museum of Fort Worth, 22, 140–141
  Museum of Science and Nature, 50–51
  Nasher Sculpture Center, 19, 62, 78–79, 81, 102

National Cowgirl Museum and Hall of Fame, 143, 144–145
North Fort Worth Historical Society, 156
Old Red Museum of Dallas County History and Culture, 26
Sid W. Richardson Collection of Western Art, 22, 133, 158
Sixth Floor Museum, 28
Trammell and Margaret Crow Collection of Asian Art, 19, 80–81
Women's Museum, 43

N
Nasher, Ray, 20, 102
Native Americans
 Cherokee, 8, 9
 Comanche, 130
 Kiowa, 130
Neighborhoods
 Bishop Arts District, 38
 Deep Ellum, 11, 22, 27
 Downtown Dallas, 6, 15, 17, 19, 21, 26, 27, 29, 30, 32, 34, 39, 44, 56, 60, 61, 63, 66, 68, 71, 72, 81, 90, 102, 106, 107, 114, 115, 118, 147
 Downtown Fort Worth, 130, 131, 132, 154, 158
 Fair Park, 19, 32, 42, 46, 47, 77, 96
 Fort Worth Stockyards National Historic District, 130, 140, 147, 152, 154, 155, 156
 Highland Park, 11, 67, 103, 106, 107
 McKinney Town Square, 125
 Munger Place, 34
 Oak Cliff, 11, 26, 38, 69, 116, 120
 Old East Dallas, 34
 Sundance Square, 22, 132–133, 134, 158
 Swiss Avenue Historic District, 34
 West End Historic District, 11, 22, 36–37, 99, 118
Newton, David, 33

O
Oswald, Lee Harvey, 21, 28–29, 71

P
Parks
 Dallas Arboretum, 111
 Dallas Heritage Village at Old City Park, 30–31
 Dallas World Aquarium and Zoological Garden, 6, 118–119
 Dallas Zoo, 120–121
 Fair Park, 10, 11, 15, 42, 44, 50, 51, 53, 115
 Fort Worth Botanic Garden, 147–148
 Fort Worth Water Gardens, 22, 63, 64, 131
 Fort Worth Zoo, 150–151
 Fountain Place, 70
 Lee Park, 115, 116
 Lone Star Park, 100–101
 Pioneer Plaza Park, 73
 Reverchon Park, 116
 Six Flags Over Texas, 22, 98, 117
 Texas Discovery Gardens, 47
 Trinity Trails, 147
 Turtle Creek, 116
 Victory Park, 29, 37, 99
 White Rock Lake, 114
Pei, I. M., 19, 70, 71, 73, 82, 83, 85
Perot, Ross, 83

R
Republic of Texas, 9, 13, 26, 106
Richardson, Sid W., 158
Rivers
 Red River, 9

Trinity River, 8, 9, 17, 29, 38, 106, 130, 147, 154
Ruby, Jack, 28, 71

S
Sports
 Dallas Cowboys, 19–21, 53, 88, 96–97
 Dallas Mavericks, 68, 99
 Dallas Stars, 99
 FC Dallas, 106
 Frisco Rough Riders, 99, 107
 Lone Star Park, 100
 Texas Rangers, 19, 21, 98–99, 117
 White Rock Marathon, 114
Stadia
 American Airlines Center, 29, 68, 99, 101
 Ameriquest Field, 98, 101
 Cotton Bowl, 19, 52, 53, 93, 96
 Texas Motor Speedway, 104–105
 Texas Stadium, 52, 88, 96–97
Statues
 Dallas Piece, The, 22, 71, 73
 Flying Pegasus, 56–57, 68
 Mustangs at Las Colinas, The, 124
 Trailing Longhorns, 22, 54–56, 73
Streets
 Akard Street, 59
 Bryan Parkway, 34
 Bryan Street, 34, 64
 Canton Street, 27
 Commerce Street, 6, 26, 27, 29, 59
 Dealey Plaza, 28–29, 63
 Elm Street, 19, 27, 28, 29, 61, 72
 Ervay Street, 64, 72
 Field Street, 61
 Gaston Avenue, 34
 Hillcrest Avenue, 103
 Main Street/Dallas, 27, 29, 62, 63, 72
 Main Street/Denton, 127
 McKinney Avenue, 67
 Pearl Street, 66, 85
 Preston Road, 106, 107
 Ross Avenue, 70, 85
 Sundance Square, 22, 132–133, 134, 158
 Swiss Avenue, 11, 34
 Thanksgiving Square, 63, 64–65
Sumners, Hatton, 26
Synagogues
 Temple Emanu-El, 64

T
Texas Ballet Theater, 44, 134
Texas Centennial Exposition, 9, 10, 11–16, 23, 30, 42, 43, 44, 45, 47, 48, 52, 77, 115, 144, 146
Texas Declaration of Independence, 125
Texas League, 98
Texas State Fair, 48–49, 52, 100
Theaters
 Billy Bob's Texas, 155
 Casa Mañana, 146
 Cowtown Coliseum, 8, 152, 154, 155, 157
 Dallas Center for the Performing Arts, 19, 44, 85
 Morton H. Meyerson Symphony Center, 19, 82–83
 Music Hall at Fair Park, 44
 Nancy Lee and Perry R. Bass Performance Hall, 22, 134
Thornton, R. L. (Mayor), 15, 42

W
Worth, William Jenkins (General), 130